Stories From the Inside Out

John, 'The Old Fella' Reed

Stories From the Inside Out

Contents

Dedication

This book is dedicated to those men who have contributed to it by talking openly about their own experiences, either from a staff perspective, or from the criminal life they have led, but now left behind.

My thanks are due to all of them, and I sincerely hope that those reading this book will understand that the Criminal Justice System we have in the UK, though better than many others around the world, is not faultless and can be improved, depending entirely upon how the public and their representatives in Government, react to a changing situation in an ever more dangerous world.

Stories From the Inside Out

Why this book had to be written

John Reed

This book has been in my mind for many a long year. Since 2016, when I first formed my community interest company I have been working in prison, with people in need of some help and support with their mental health.

Mental health in prison is a serious problem and by taking a friendly voice, and a friendly face into prison we find that the men respond positively. Many men in prison will suffer from mental illness. It may be as simple as depression or anxiety. Which can lead to self-harm, and even suicide. The problem is in their mind and if we can overcome that problem then we can reduce those activities that nobody wants to see.

Poetry in prison is a simple solution. A way of bringing an interest to the men, which we call a "therapeutic intervention". By guiding the residents through the process of creative writing they learn to write a poem. I show them examples of poetry that I've written. I lead by example, and that creates a trust and respect between us that helps reduce the problems they are experiencing.

This book details conversations that I have had with many men in prison. And we talk about their situation. How they got there and what they hope to learn while they're in prison. All of these things, to an outsider, maybe alien. But to somebody on the inside. they are very important factors in their life.

Some mental health problems can only be overcome with drugs and treatments. Equally some mental health problems can be reduced or eradicated with a friendly voice. This book will seek to show you how the men in prison react when we speak to them, when we treat them as people and not as prisoners. And when we take a small piece of the outside, inside.

Stories From the Inside Out

About the Author

My name is John Reed and I am the author of this book which is intended to show the plight of the prisoner inside any prison. My story is a long one because I am past retirement age. However, at the end of my working life, I have found a passion, I have found a topic that really interests me.

Let me tell you something about myself. At the time of writing, I'm 76 years of age. And I've worked all of my life since leaving school at the age of 15. I left school and became an apprentice in a nationalised industry, the gas industry. And there I remained until I had completed my five years apprenticeship.

In 1970, I married for the first time and over the next 10 years my wife and I welcomed two sons into the world. In 1980. I moved home from Surrey to Worcestershire. The marriage did not last, and in 1984 I remarried. I have been married to Diane ever since.

Over these many years I have had lots of changes to my career. This is because I have always wanted a job that can earn me enough money to maintain a good family life. To provide for my wife and children and a job that I could enjoy.

Then, in 2016, a man came in to my life and changed it forever. That man was Andy Mullaney[1].

I am firm believer in fate. And I believe that Andy came into my life for a reason. We met at a networking meeting and he started to persuade me that I should establish a community interest company. At this point I had no idea what CIC was but research told me this was a good thing to do. And I believed that fate had delivered to me a future, a future that I firmly embraced and have continued with ever since.

The purpose of my community interest company is to help people

---

[1] Andy Mullaney is a Midlands based author. His book, Didn't Anyone Ever Tell You? It's All A Game!! Provides the basis of his work leveraging networks for positive change along with bespoke consultancy services tailored to individuals, businesses, charities, and public bodies alike. Irrespective of age or tenure, he provides support, advice, and guidance to navigate diverse challenges.

overcome loneliness. But more than that, the problems associated or emanating from. Loneliness; depression, anxiety, low self-esteem and much more.

Try to imagine living alone. Very few people come into your life, you suffer loneliness which previously in your life had never been a factor. If you were experiencing this in a normal situation that would be a problem, but one which has multiple avenues of support to overcome. You would have the freedom to make choices.

Now give some consideration to prison. Imagine that you are locked in a cell, measuring maybe 12 feet by 6 feet. You are alone, you may only leave that cell for two hours every day. For company, you have a television. If you are lucky, you may have a radio. You will eat your meals in that cell. You will sleep in that cell. You will use the toilet in that cell. You will keep all of your possessions in that cell.

Things could be worse. Imagine, if you were sharing that cell with another person. They could be a complete stranger. They may be a dangerous person. It is possible that you have no common interests. That you do not even enjoy the same TV programmes. Their personal habits drive you insane and compromise is not in their vocabulary. And yet you are living with that person for perhaps 22 hours every day, seven days per week…for years. Maybe now you can understand why mental health issues occur so often in prison and are a problem for so many.

The people I talk about in this book are real people, living in this way, and it is really important for society to understand that we need to change the criminal justice system, and the lifestyle imposed on prisoners, so that it serves society better in the future.

The process I use to overcome mental health problems is called "therapeutic intervention". Put simply we have a way of improving the mental health of the people that we deal with. But we cannot do this without their trust and respect in us. Similarly, we must demonstrate to them that we respect their situation, and that we trust them. The question therefore becomes, 'How do you develop a friendship with a person in prison?'. Let me explain;

As I meet any new group I greet them with a firm handshake, a smile and then a welcome. As they enter the room, I only know one thing, that we are going to share some poetry together. Many of the people have written poetry for many years. Conversely, many have never written one in their life. They only have one thing in common. They're all residents in the same prison. They may know each other. Or they may not. They may be friends, or they may not.

Some people cannot read or write but members of the group will help them. And so, the idea of writing a poem begins to gel in their mind. I explain that the poem we're going to write can be about anything. It is a way of expressing themselves; any complaints can be written in a poem. We discuss the topics and we chat and we enjoy each other's company. During our time together we share a cup of tea, we share biscuits, we laugh, and gradually we become friends. A unique type of friendship yes, but still friends.

Helping inmates to write, and read, is just one small way that I help them to become more useful to society, as well as improving their mental health whilst still inside.

But we forget that within the prison system there are many people with a huge array of skills and expertise that could be of major benefit to the country as a whole. However, we tend to ignore this volume of skills, providing no focus or application in rehabilitation, and when we release these people they often settle back into their old ways.

The stories you are about to read are all true. They are the stories told by the people that I have met in prison. These are real people, with real problems. There are also people that have written poetry for me and in return, I have written poetry for them. As a group, we have got to know each other, over time trust and respect has grown. And this has an astonishing positive impact on their mental health.

Rather than suffer in silence, the pain of loneliness, they begin to open up and tell me their worries? Of course I cannot resolve all of the problems, but I can listen, I can sympathise, and in some cases, I can take action that will save their lives. This statement sounds very bold but it is true, and based on experience I believe that a problem shared is a problem halved. And so, by listening to the men I can help them resolve their problems and improve their lives.

My own frustrations, how many? As I've already said, I believe in fate but what a shame that this idea, this concept, this plan for my life did not happen at a younger age. It is hard to know, indeed impossible, how many years I have left to write about the people that mean so much to me in my life.

However, while I still have the ability to write about this, then I will. The topic is vitally important. Society needs to understand how important changing the way we treat prisoners in this country is, how this change can result in benefits not just to those inmates but to society in general.

In helping them, we help us.

I hope that by reading this book. You will become more understanding of what we as a society can do in the future. This country spends a lot of money on locking people up. This money could be reduced dramatically if we adopted a different stance. Put simply, we should be rehabilitating people rather than simply removing them from society.

Certainly, there are people in prison who should stay there, for a long time, perhaps forever, because the severity of their crime was so bad. Those that would be a danger to society if they were released. But they represent a tiny percentage of the total held.

Rehabilitation should be the core focus of incarceration. Prison should be a place of retraining, a place of fresh starts, a place where people can learn to be better people. Until it is we shall continue to pay a very high price.

Note that names and other details have been changed to protect the identity of individuals throughout this book.

Stories From the Inside Out

Foreword

I am incredibly proud, privileged, and humbled to write this foreword. John's passion for alleviating loneliness—especially in prisons—is not only inspiring but profoundly necessary.

John is one of life's true givers. If he were family, he'd be your favourite uncle or brother. In my case, as we're not related, he's simply a remarkable friend. His generosity of spirit knows no bounds, and this book is an extension of that—a gift that reveals the unseen stories behind lives we are often too quick to judge.

Through John, I've learned not just about prisons, but about myself—about the biases I didn't realise I held and the assumptions we so easily make about who "deserves" help. John has never been incarcerated, yet he has spent countless hours inside prison walls, offering companionship, learning, and support to those who are often forgotten. His ability to see beyond judgment is a lesson to us all. He understands that not everyone is willing—or able—to cross that threshold. But what he asks, and what this book invites, is that we listen to the stories told in a series of interviews.

That we think with consideration. That we see the full story.

And that's why this book is so important. It opens a window into a world we rarely witness, yet one we often feel entitled to judge. Ask yourself: Where do my opinions on prison and those inside come from? The media? A headline? A story from a friend of a friend?

John once told me, "We are all just one mistake away from being in prison ourselves." Think about that. How many of us have driven distracted, had a near miss, made a reckless choice in the heat of the moment? Many good people now live behind bars—not because they are inherently bad, but because of a split-second decision with life-altering consequences.

These stories matter. They are written in a way that allows you to read at your own pace—pick it up, put it down, reflect, return. Or, if you're like me, you'll likely devour it in one sitting. However you choose to read it, I urge you to share it. Buy a copy for a friend, a colleague, or someone who might need a shift in perspective. Because knowledge is power—and this book is rich with it.

Yes, some parts will be uncomfortable. But John is your guide, offering you the same protection and understanding he gives to those he supports. Trust him. You'll come away changed.

And here's a final thought. If you don't know John, please reach out—through a review of this book or personally. There are few people like him in this world, and that is a pity. If there were more, we'd see a world with greater love, compassion, joy, respect, and appreciation for one another.

More people would choose the path of kindness, be more aware of each other's needs, and—who knows—perhaps fewer lives would be lost to society. More talent would flourish, and more people would give selflessly, just as John does every day.

Andy Mullaney

2/25

Chapter 1

Les

Let's begin with a bit of background.

I, with my friend and ex-con Ed Flannagan, decided that recording interviews with inmates, during our work in the prisons, would be a great way to capture their stories and in turn help us everyday folk to gain a little more insight into prison life.

The first of these interviews was with Les. He was a prisoner on the Vulnerable Prisoners Unit (VP) in a men's prison in the Midlands. His crime is irrelevant, as is that of every prisoner we spoke to. What we are focusing on here is gaining an insight into prison life so that we may begin to consider how improvements there can help reduce the number of people being in there (especially repeat offenders) and support real rehabilitation.

Now I also want to stress that yes, these are real people, with hopes, dreams, families, etc. but they have done wrong and that usually means that there are victims of their crimes. I have every sympathy with those victims, I do not intend to lessen the impact of the crimes on those people and I absolutely agree that justice must be served and punishment be imposed upon the criminal.

This book, and my mission, is all about preventing more crime through rehabilitation and that has to begin by treating inmates like normal people (which they most often are) and doing all we can to return them as law abiding and useful members of society upon their release.

It begins by listening to their stories so that we might understand them better.

Let me draw a picture for you. My contributor and I are both at ease, he is in his wheel chair and I am sitting on his bed, there being no other chairs available. Close by we have a sound recordist and his assistant, there to record every word my man utters.

The atmosphere is very warm, I have known all of those present for some time, and we all know why we are gathered here today.

My resident of this prison is rather special to me, we have shared many a conversation and I know how his mind works. What I do not know is why he is in here, what crime has he been found guilty of ? Neither do I need or want to know, although unusually for me I know he will never be released, as the following conversation will reveal.

I begin by exploring how he coped after the judge said, "take him down" (or do they really say that ? I don't know actually).

What you are about to read is my friends account of what happened on the day he was sent to prison for the first time in his life, at a very advanced age.

The Interview . . .

JR: Hello, this is John the storyteller fella talking on the landings with a man living in his pad and talking about old age. *What's it like growing old in prison?* Les is in his upper 70s and he's serving quite a sentence in here. So, his thoughts on his life are going to be really interesting. Good afternoon, Les:

Les: Good afternoon, John.

JR: Pleased to meet you and I've met you on very many occasions. You are an old friend, a trusted friend and somebody I think an awful lot of.

Les: And we consider you to be a very good person within the jail. And this is all the inmates that say that same thing.

JR: Have they had a vote on it?

Les: Yeah.

JR: Well, that hasn't sent me the results.

Les: No, well, we're going to hang you, but don't worry about it.

JR: Okay. All right, well, I'll try and survive that then. Okay. On a serious note, Les, you and I have discussed this more than once. So, you know and I know that your life will end in here because the sentence you have is longer than the life expectancy.

Les: My life expectancy, yes.

JR: And I don't wish to make too big a thing of it, but it's the real world, isn't it?

Les: It is, definitely.

JR: And this is your first sentence? It is.

Les: It is. I've never been in any kind of problem, trouble or anything throughout the whole of my life.

JR: So, this must have been as a terrible shock when you were in court and sent down.

Les: Yes.

JR: What were you thinking?

Les: I actually thought this is the end.

JR: Did you?

Les: I actually thought that this is the end.

JR: The end of your life, you mean?

Les: The end of my life, yeah. Having said that, I had the support of my family, which was fantastic.

JR: And made the difference?

Les: It made a tremendous difference, yeah. I found that life within here wasn't quite as bad as what I thought it would be.

JR: Well, that's one of the reasons we're doing these interviews, because very few people on the outside know what it's like on the inside. And the only way you're going to get a picture of it is to talk to the people 'living that dream', perhaps some would say. And there are many out there that would say, they've done the crime, lock them up, throw away the key.

Les: I know. Yeah.

JR: So, is it a society within a society?

Les: It's definitely that.

JR: So, you thought this was the end? As you travelled in that vehicle from court to prison, when you arrived here, what happened?

Les: First off, I was searched completely. And then I was told to strip off totally.

JR: That was a pretty sight, I bet.

Les: Yeah. Wonderful sight, really. And then I was given prison clothes to wear. They even checked my hearing aids. In case there was something in there. And then we had to go through the X-ray machine, followed by being put into a waiting room. And I was in the waiting room then for about two and a half hours.

JR: Okay. And were you alone or was there a crowd of you?

Les: I was alone.

JR: Alone?

Les: Yeah.

JR: That must have been scary?

Les: Yes, it was quite scary. Especially when you've got other prisoners coming by and they're banging on the windows and that kind of thing.

JR: Being nasty? Because there's an inherent belief, isn't there, that people in the Vulnerable Prisoner Unit (VP) are entirely different to everybody else and other people will despise you for being on the VP.

Les: That's very true. The only thing is, at that time, they didn't know. No one knew who I was or what I was or what anything at all. Only once you come to the wing itself that you're known as whatever.

JR: You know I do a lot of stuff with loneliness and it strikes me from what you just said. But that must have been the loneliest part of the journey, surely?

Les: Probably. The thing is, in the van that brought me here, I was locked inside a little tiny cubby hole. And I could hardly get my legs out.

JR: Does it have a seatbelt?

Les: No. No. It's strange. You think it would, wouldn't you?

JR: You would have thought so, yes. Okay. In two and a half hours, what happens then?

Les: Then I had to go through an interview with a nurse and she was very nice and very understanding, explained lots of different things to me on the medical side. So that was all quite good. Then the next thing was to go to the reception counter. We would go to that reception counter, deposit all the clothes and things that you carried in with you and then you were shipped off to your cell or I was shipped off to my cell. And I arrived in my cell at 7.40 in the evening. I'd left the court just after one o'clock.

JR: Goodness me. So, it's a long afternoon.

Les: A very long afternoon.

JR: Can we spend a brief moment talking about the condition of your body, the health problems that you've got? Because I can see, for example, that you've got hearing aids the same as I have. So, we're both of us to get into an age where we need a bit of help with our listening. But I know you've got more than that, haven't you?

Les: Yeah. Quite a bit more.

JR: You're not too embarrassed to tell us what it is that you're suffering from?

Les: No. I've got no problem telling you anything that you want to ask. I've got COPD. I've got... Shall I start at the top and work down? So, I've got a serious problem with my throat, which is number one. Then I've got a very bad cough, which is caused by my lungs. Two problems with the lungs. Serious scarring. And I can't think that they call it. An inability to work. And then I've also got bad heart. I've got liver problems and kidney problems. Enlarged prostate. Arthritis. There's another thing I can't think of the name of it.

JR: I don't wish to embarrass you, but you are a little overweight, aren't you? Just a little. A couple of pounds, I would say.

Les: I would say. If only. I would say more like sort of 24 to 30 pounds.

JR: It begs the question. So, you come into induction. You spend however long, two weeks is it normally in there, and then you get sent to the wing. You're going to need medical care, not only at that point, but for the rest of your life, aren't you? Tell me about the medical care in this prison.

Les: When I first came in, I had the induction thing with the nurse, which was very good. She was very understanding and everything was explained by her. I went to the induction wing and I was there then for six days only. Normally, they have two weeks. Because it was so bad with COVID, I don't know why it was, but they moved me on. I had COVID twice while I've been in here. So, but I survived that. I've had pneumonia twice since I've been in here. I've had a heart attack since I've been in here. So, yeah, there's quite a few different things that's gone on.

JR: So, hence our conversations regarding when the end comes, what happens. And it's not a conversation that you generally would have. But I think to people listening to this podcast, it will be a topic they've never even thought of. People dying in prison, but they do. And what a lonely place to die in many ways depends how and when, I suppose.

Les: Well, it does. I mean, I've got no worries about dying. None whatsoever. If I was to drop down dead right now, I've got no problem.

JR: Well, I hope you don't before we finish our interview!

Les: No, exactly. We must finish the interview first.

JR: But does that come from your faith?

Les: I'm not sure, to be honest with you.

JR: Or is it just a pragmatic view?

Les: I think it's probably, yeah. I think it's just the view that it's inevitably happens to all of us.

JR: So, you have been a regular churchgoer.

Les: Yeah. I've always had a belief there somewhere. Oh, definitely. Yeah. I mean, I've always had a belief in religion. My original belief was actually of the American Native Indians.

JR: Oh, go on. Yeah, that's a different kind of faith to what I was thinking.

Les: But at the same time, I was regularly at church as a child. So, yeah, it sort of mingled.

JR: Did that provide a good foundation, or as it's now coming out, was the church not entirely guilt-free when it comes to looking after church goers?

Les: My church was definitely not guilt-free. The preacher there, we had to make sure his private parts were clean.

JR: So, it wasn't pleasant?

Les: No, no. Far from it.

JR: I suppose some people would say, well, maybe that was where the rot set in, I don't mean to be unkind, but some people would argue that their childhood trauma is something to carry right through their life. And eventually, it gets them.

Les: Yeah, definitely.

JR: Who knows? I don't. I've not been subjected to it myself.

Les: I would agree 100% on that.

JR: Would you?

Les: Yes, definitely.

JR: It's a shame, though, isn't it?

Les: It is. I mean, I went through all kinds of abuse, sexual, physical, mental, right up until I was just around 16 and managed to leave home.

JR: That's a few weeks ago now, isn't it!! Yes, I don't want to give your exact age away.

Les: It's sort of the 60 years and a few weeks. Yeah? So... Yeah, something like that. Yeah. Yeah, that's okay.

JR: What an interesting life, but not entirely without his problems, is it? Because we finish up at the end of the day, not how you would have hoped your life to be. This, I know is a very difficult topic, but financially, you had made provision for your retirement very adequately. And I think it's true to say you no longer have access to that money.

Les: I have no access whatsoever to any of my cash.

JR: So, you'd have a reason to feel bitter?

Les: Very. I am very bitter regarding the government pension. So, I've worked 60 years paying taxes right up until two days after I came in here. You know...

JR: And you don't get a pension in here?

Les: And I don't get any pension. I now get £2.50 a week. It's very generous, isn't it?

JR: And again, you know, people listen to this. £2.50. What can you buy for £2.50?

Les: You can't buy anything.

JR: In prison, you have a kind of a canteen system, they call it, don't they?

Les: That's correct.

JR: And canteen day is Friday. Yes. So how does that work, then? You place an order?

Les: Well, yes. You're given a sheet with all the different things on that you can purchase.

JR: But with £2.50, is there much that you can buy?

Les: With £2.50, there's nothing that I can buy.

JR: So, what happens? You let the £2.50 mount up for a few weeks? But what kind of thing do you need to buy?

Les: Well, it's the odd thing like biscuits or coffee. Treats. mostly treats.

Yeah. Liquorice All Sorts? Yeah, liquorice. I wish! They don't have Liquorice All Sorts on our account.

JR: No, but I know you get them through a sort of vicarious route. I know you do. So, let's try and describe the conditions you're living under now, because very few people have been in a prison cell And people reading your story, they might be very interested to know. So, when I first knew you on this wing, you weren't in this particular cell, were you?

Les: No, I wasn't.

JR: The cell you were in was very much smaller; half the size. It was a single cell with just you in it. In that cell was a small table top for you to put a few pieces on, including your television set, and you had a toilet and a wash basin. So, they could have locked the doors, and other than feed you, they could have left you locked in there forever. And it seems to me that you almost were, because the wheelchair, which you're currently sitting in and need to use all the time, wouldn't go through the door to get you out onto the landing, would it?

Les: That's correct. That's correct.

JR: But when we first met, you were coming to my poetry course and climbing the stairs; not anymore.

Les: No. When I first came in, I was just using walking stick. The healthcare here is so poor that I went downhill fast. Really fast. So, I don't really know whether to say anything about the healthcare, because it really is a poor system, very, very poor.

JR: It's not good, not good enough?

Les: No, no. Definitely not.

JR: But I came in one day, and you weren't here. And when I inquired where you were, they said he's in hospital. You were away for two weeks. That costs the prison an awful lot of money, didn't it? Because you have to have you guarded.

Les: They have four guards, 24 hours a day. Yeah.

JR: Now, to me, that's utterly ridiculous. Given your health, and your age, and your ability to run. It seems to me that you're not the most difficult person to guard. You're not likely to put your running shoes on and go, are you?. They put someone with you all the time. And whatever happens to you in that prison, the prison guard witnesses.

Les: In the hospital, you mean?

JR: In the hospital, sorry. Yeah. It's as simple as that, isn't it?

Les: Yeah, it is.

JR: But when you came back, it was an ill wind that blows cold, wasn't it? Because you found yourself in the pad that you're now in.

Les: No. No, no, no. No? I still went back to my single cell. Oh, I'm sorry. Yes. Yes, I went back to my small single cell. Right. And stayed there for further, oh, eight or nine months. Okay. And then, it's only just recently, something like eight, ten weeks ago, that I moved into this larger cell. Right. Whereas I'm now able to get out of the door, which is kept open quite a lot now, compared to being locked away for 23 hours a day.

JR: And how much improvement is that on your life?

Les: It's a great mental improvement.

JR: Right. Because men come in and chat, do they?

Les: They do, yeah.

JR: I certainly do. But other men do as well. And quite often, there's two or three in here, and you're having...

Les: Very often, yes. Putting the world to right, I think, is probably what people would call it.

JR: That's what people would call it. And luckily, humour pervades all the way through, doesn't it?

Les: It does.

JR: Because it has to.

Les: What you find is, people laugh on the outside and cry on the inside.

JR: Which is a natural reaction to the environment we're in.

Les: Yes, I think so.

JR: And I don't think that's ever going to change, is it?

Les: No.

JR: So, as I look around me, what have we got? We've got a room that measures, what, roughly?

Les: 10 feet square.

JR: 10 feet square, roughly. It has a toilet and a wash basin hidden behind the curtain. It has a bed. With a tilting section on one end, is it?

Les: Yes. That's special for me, though. Yeah. Not everyone gets that.

JR: There is a desktop with a television on it. It's got all your, what should we call it, all your bits and pieces, I suppose, is a polite way. Some Bisto I can see there, a little carton of milk, a drink, some cutlery, plastic cutlery. That's your medicine supply over there by the looks of it. Drainage, draining bags.

Les: My diabetes. All the stuff you go with it. Oh, I forgot to mention diabetes.

JR: You left it off the list.

Les: Yeah.

JR: I think we're now into double figures, then, as to what's wrong with you. Yeah. But your humour hasn't gone, has it?

Les: No, I've tried to keep it on.

JR: That's when I'll know you're dead. Yeah. Because you won't take the mickey out of me.

Les: I'll try not to. I might come back and haunt you a bit though.

JR: Well, you might. Who knows what's going to happen. Yeah, exactly, yeah. But how could we summarise this, then, Les? We could say, here is a man facing adversity with a smile on his face. Yes. He still has opinions. Yeah. He still has loves in his life. He still has the ability to chatter. He has lots of things. But what he doesn't have is his freedom.

Les: That's the most important one.

JR: Now, what is a prison about? It's about taking away your freedom. So to that extent, society's taking its revenge on whatever you were found guilty of doing?

Les: That's what it is. It is actually revenge. Yes.

JR: However, is there a reason why your health care shouldn't be as good as it is on the outside? I don't think so, in fact it's counterproductive as when prisoners do become ill the costs of treatment can be enormous.

Les: There isn't any reason whatsoever, we find that the health care within this prison is extremely poor. Extremely poor.

JR: But it's nothing to do with the people.

Les: It's to do with the organisation of the health care system. Today, I've just been to the hospital to have my hearing checked and the hearing aids reset. It doesn't work very well, but it's been done. I had these hearing aids about six months ago, approximately. And prior to that, I had no hearing aids for 16 months, none whatsoever.

JR: Was that better? You couldn't hear me?

Les: Yeah. Everyone kept saying, you know, repeat it. But the health care side of it really is very, very poor. I think what they believe is, because you're a prisoner, you're making things up just to get out of the prison.

JR: I can't comment I have no idea. I don't experience it so I don't know.. And it does seem to me that you were missing from here from about 10 o'clock this morning until three o'clock this afternoon, something like that. If I was getting my hearing aids checked, I'd pop in the opticians, it'd be done in five minutes. So, to that extent, yeah, the health system has got a lot to answer for. But as a person confined to a wheelchair, they first of all got to get you down the ground floor where the vehicle is to take you to the hospital. That's no small challenge, is it?

Les: No, because there is no, most of the time there is no lift.

JR: Okay. So they take you there, then they've got to assign a vehicle and an escort to take you to the hospital. Yeah. They've got a park. They've got to stay with you. You've got to go in and see the hearing aid man, which might take 10 minutes.

Les: No, and they have to come in as well. They're not allowed to leave your side.

JR: Again, in case you run away. Yeah. I don't think it's very likely Les to be honest. But remember, rules is rules, and that's the way it operates.

Les: Well, that's the way it is.

JR: And prisons couldn't work without rules.

Les: I think we have to accept that. Yeah. We have to accept the fact that it is prison. It's a place where you're locked up. The whole environment is built around the law of the prison. So you have to just accept whatever it is, which I do accept.

JR: If I came in to see you in 10 years' time, how unlikely that might sound.

Les: That's very unlikely. I won't be alive then.

JR: If I came in to see you in 10 years' time and you were looking back on 12 years or more in this prison, what would your major focus be?

What was the main memory you would take with you?

Les: Well, I think once again, I'd say the healthcare. Healthcare and education. They're the two things that are really lacking.

JR: I was hoping for a positive response, something like, I've made some really good friends in here.

Les: Oh, right. The men in here helped me. I've received tremendous amounts of help from other prisoners, that is. I've also had quite a lot of help from some of the officers. Yes. Some of them are absolutely fantastic. Okay. And others not so good. Okay.

JR: Well, that's life, isn't it?

Les: That's normal life, isn't it?

JR: Wherever you work, people are like that. Yeah.

Les: And wherever you go outdoors, you know, anywhere that you go, it's always the same. You meet people that you like, you meet people that you don't like, meet some people that will help and other people that will just walk on by.

JR: Exactly right. But let me repeat the question but in another way. Looking back on your life today, you've had more than your three school years and ten, we both know that. Yeah. What's your happiest memory?

Les: My happiest memory? Oh, there's a lot of them. There's a lot of them.

JR: Do they all focus on family?

Les: Yes, definitely. 100%. 100%. My first wife, absolutely wonderful, fantastic. And I couldn't fault her. But then we divorced. She wanted to divorce and that was it. And then my partner that I have now for 27, yeah, 27 and a half years, she is wonderful, all her family, fantastic people, very well educated.

JR: Could we say then, if you die tomorrow and I hope you don't, I sincerely hope you don't, you would take with you some very happy memories of a life that's well lived.

Les: Yes.

JR: Just sadness that it finished up the way it did.

Les: It's the ending is the problem.

JR: I can see that.

....

At the end of our chat Les wanted to talk about the poetry that he had created as a result of my visits and sessions with the inmates. Les made his own book. It took him hours and hours. And when he showed it to me, I offered to improve it, not by changing the content, but simply by printing it. And I did print it all out for him you know.

He and I have a unique relationship, a real friendship. And I put the book together for him. I printed out every poem that he'd ever written, and then I wrote a poem back to him. And it left some spare pages. So, he wrote some more poetry, and I typed it up and bought it in, and it left one page empty. And only this morning, I've come in with a little poem that he wrote, and I've put a picture of Les on the bottom. So, he can put the book, and the book is complete.

....

Les: One thing I would like to say before you go before you cut off is that without you, a lot of these guys in here would never have learned to read and write or to write poems. And you have been so good to us. That's been great. It really has been great. And I wish I could read my poem about you.

JR: Have you got the book there?

Les: Yes, I've got my books in there.

JR: Which one is this, Les? Show me.

Les: This is *We Want John.*

JR: Oh, OK. Go on then.

Les: And this is the one that's been spread all over the prison. It does. So we'll kick off. Tit**les:** being *We Want John*.

> *One day I was sat here, in my cell, contemplating this life of hell.*
>
> *When along came Mr. Marge, an officer, and cracked a cracking joke.*
>
> *We're going to start a poetry class, and I think you're just the bloke.*
>
> *I laughed so much I nearly peed. But after a chat, I agreed.*

*Then came the first Tuesday morning, not sure of what to
expect.*

I asked an officer at 10.30, why are we so late?

Whoa, whoa, he said. Don't get your knickers in a twist.

Why are you complaining? You're not on the list.

Eventually I made it. It's being run by this old man.

*He told us there's nothing you can't do, and all the things
you can.*

We started by writing a poem. Everyone suggested a line.

Continue until we finished, although it took some time.

*Now we've come to our last day. Six weeks have passed so
quick.*

We all wish it could continue. Yes, we all want it to last.

As John Reed, the old fella, has taught us all so well,

*we want to learn so much more, and the whole wide world,
to tell.*

JR: So that's why I call street poetry. Now, the main purpose of this
book was I suppose Les that it gave you an enormous amount of pleasure
putting it together.

Les: Fantastic amount.

JR: And when that terrible day comes, and you leave here in a box,
somebody will get all your belongings, including the book.

Les: They will.

JR: And they'll be able to see what you did while you were in here.
When you got private time, on your own.

Les: Yes, because it has been, it really has been an eye-opener to me.

JR: Has it been? Since I've been coming in the role I've fulfilled, you
know I've enjoyed it so much. Yes. I just love it. And have you got my
poem that I wrote to you?

Les: Yes, I have.

JR: I'll read it out to you.

Les: Okay

JR: The heading is *A tribute to Mr L*.

> *Dear Les, I so much enjoy your company. You never get the hump with me.*
>
> *Each day when we chat about this and that, your comments on life let me know where you're at.*
>
> *I remember the day we first met on the wing, to my poetry class, much fun did you bring.*
>
> *The men all applauded your skill with the words. Each line you wrote, it was never absurd.*
>
> *My memories of you are etched deep in my mind. The pleasure you gave to me, never easy to find.*
>
> *Now I know you broke the law, but in my world, well, that's not a chore.*
>
> *To see you now, happy, cheerful, and all smiles, and in your new pad, much roomier and with style.*
>
> *It's true this prison is not the ritz, but for now, at least, you're not frozen to bits.*
>
> *So keep smiling, my friend, right up to the end, and remember me always as your friend.*
>
> *For I know that in time we shall both depart, but for now, just smile and keep a good heart.*

Les: Thank you.

JR: This is the one I did this morning, that you wrote this special one.

Les: Okay, so, very short poem that I wrote in a matter of 15 minutes, and it's called *Please Repeat*:

> *I'm sat here in solitary, all day, every day.*
>
> *No one stops to chat no more, I have nothing left to say.*
>
> *But when they do, I'm in a stew, as I can't hear a word.*
>
> *For over a year I've needed, new hearing aids, it really is absurd.*

…….

And finally, our conversation turned to the only green thing in the cell:

Les: Two years and three months old, it started as an orange seed. The prison provided us with fruit. I took three seeds from the orange and grew all three of them. Two other prisoners had the plants when they left here to go home, and this one, which is now almost two and a half years old, it will fruit when it's six years old.

JR: Can I have the orange off it then?

Les: Yeah, yeah.

JR: Because you won't be here for it, will you?

Les: I'm not allowed to take it with me to another prison.

JR: All that's left for me to say really is, Les, you know what I think of you. I really enjoyed the conversation. I hope this goes down as a conversation for people to remember, because growing old in prison is something that more and more people will have to face. And that's because historic crimes are being fetched into court that were committed 30, 40 years ago. People are living longer, and judges are handing out longer sentences. So, it's inevitable that the number of older people, and we know it's the fastest growing group in prison today, we know that it can only get worse. So, thank you very much for your time, sir. I've really enjoyed our conversation.

Les: So have I.

Chapter 2

Leon

Leon's story is one of transformation. A soldier who dedicated twelve years of his life to serving in the British Army, Leon saw combat in Iraq and Afghanistan.

Like many veterans, he returned home carrying more than just memories—he brought back the weight of experiences that reshaped his view of the world and, ultimately, himself. What followed was a struggle with mental health, addiction, and the difficulty of transitioning back into civilian life.

His story is not just about the impact of war but about finding a way to rebuild. In this conversation, Leon opens up about his time in the military, the challenges he faced after leaving, and how prison—an unexpected detour—became the place where he started to put his life back together.

The Interview . . .

JR: So, let's take you back to the start. Let's take you back to your childhood, growing up, family environment. Where are we, mum and dad?

Leon: Yeah, yeah.

JR: Brothers, sisters?

Leon: One brother.

JR: And life was good?

Leon: It was.

JR: Life was fine. You went to a normal school?

Leon: Absolutely. Absolutely standard.

JR: And what age did you leave school?

Leon: 16 and three quarters.

JR: Yeah, so you didn't stay on for A-levels or anything like that?

Leon: No.

JR: Was that always the ambition?

Leon: It was.

JR: How do you, when you consider the army as a career, how do you decide which part of the army you want to go in?

Leon: Well, initially when I went to do my barbed test at the careers office, I was going to join the infantry. 9-11 had just happened, fancy getting into the fight but my test results showed a higher level of soldier that I could have been, so they was pushing for the Royal Electrical and Mechanical Engineers.

But when I initially went to do that, I injured my knee and I had to wait an extra 12 months while it healed before I rejoined. And I had to go back and redo it and I ended up joining the Royal Regiment of Fusiliers.

JR: Okay, so there's somebody like me that's got no idea of all these different regiments and things. Where do they fit into the scheme of things?

Leon: So, the Royal Electrical and Mechanical Engineers, they mainly do vehicle maintenance, electrical wiring bases or fixing the machinery etc and the Fusiliers are an infantry battalion.

JR: Do they go to war?

Leon: Yes.

JR: To support what's happening?

Leon: Yes.

JR: Okay, so how long before you went to war?

Leon: I did two years of training until I was over the age of 18 and my first war I did was Iraq.

JR: We've all seen it on the television, but really got no idea of the reality of it until we talked to somebody like you that can define what the reality of it is. So, let's start at the beginning. When they told you that you were going to Iraq, were you scared or excited or both or what?

Leon: I think most soldiers tell you they're not scared when they first go to a war zone, it's a lot easier.

The first two weeks, I'm not going to lie, I was terrified. You very very quickly become used to that situation and kind of fit into that sort of lifestyle and I think in a way it changes you. It's not normal to see people shooting at you or your mates being shot, or innocent people being shot. It's all very strange.

The images that go in, what you see, what you've done, where you've been, it doesn't go out of your head. You very quickly go from being a scared teenager to having to grow up very very quickly.

JR: And it's all a bit difficult.

Leon: Yeah.

JR: Yeah, it's quite a big change. So do you literally get off the plane, into the barracks, and the next day you're out fighting, or how does it work?

Leon: Pretty much. So you land in the country, get a day or two to set up, and then briefed on what patrols and missions you'll be doing, and then pretty much out on the ground.

JR: Talk me through an average day, please, you know, from getting up to going to bed.

Leon: So obviously we'll wake up, breakfast, shave, shower, three S's before I mention the other one. Yeah, get packed ready for the day, get briefing, get out on the ground.

JR: Is the briefing the point where you learn what you're going to do that day?

Leon: Yeah, pretty much the briefing you're going to take, what you're looking out for. So you've got an objective, and it's objective driven.

JR: And somebody higher up than you decides what those objectives are.

Leon: Correct.

JR: Okay, so you're armed? What are you carrying on your person?

Leon: So we had a SA-80 assault rifle, and at the time we were carrying a 6mm, 9mm pistol. Various grenades.

JR: Are there different types of grenades?

Leon: Oh yeah, you've got lethal type, which are fragmentation grenades, we have thunder flashes, which cause a distraction, smoke grenades for concealment and bugging out the situation if we need to.

JR: So essentially, you know what you're doing, you're going out there, and the old thing about shoot or be shot, is the overriding in your mind?

Leon: No, basically, we don't just shoot at anyone there, you've got to obviously positively identify your target, make sure to carry a weapon.

When I was out there, you weren't allowed to fire that weapon unless fired upon. So you could see people walking around with weapons, but if they didn't shoot it, yeah. It's fair enough, just walk on by.

JR: And how do you think the local population took this when you were on patrol?

Leon: You've seen it on the TV news, haven't you, where you've got half a dozen blokes. There was people obviously happy to see us there, because obviously we're stopping the tyrants in their country basically, doing what they want to do.

JR: But do they all see them as tyrants?

Leon: Not all of them. No, but some of the tyrants are going to be amongst them.

JR: It must be a very strange environment. Now what about the weather, what time of year were you there?

Leon: Summer.

JR: So it's hot. Very hot. And you're fully kitted in an army uniform. Protective vests and all the rest of it. Helmets, heavy boots. So you've got to be physically very strong.

Leon: Yes, and mentally.

JR: And mentally, and which is the more important?

Leon: Mentally

JR: I thought you'd say that, because I know what it's led to, and I know what we're coming to at the end there.

I would think the vast majority of the people reading this would say exactly the same. Hats off to you for defending our beliefs, really, our country. So I hold you in tremendous respect.

And not only you, but anybody that's served in this dimension. So you're in Iraq. You're away from your family. You obviously are with a load of mates, because you gel into a team, you get to know each other. They're more like family.

Leon: Yes.

JR: And how long are you there for?

Leon: Six months at a time, with a two-week respite in between when we come home.

JR: They call it R&R.

Leon: Yep. And so they'll fly you home. You can go back to your family, spend a fortnight with them, and then turn around and go back and do it all again.

JR: And how long did that go on for?

Leon: Six months.

JR: How many six-month cycles?

Leon: You do one six-month cycle as a tour.

JR: Okay. Within that six months, you'll get two weeks off, and then the rest of the tour back then. Okay. Would you then do another tour the same year?

Leon: No, not usually.

JR: And life returns to normal, whatever normal is, we don't really know.

Leon: Correct.

JR: Okay. So how many years did you serve in the army?

Leon: Twelve years.

JR: So it was a real lifetime commitment at that stage of your life, wasn't it?

Leon: Yes.

JR: And coming out, what decided you to leave?

Leon: So, by the time I'd come out, and through war zones, unfortunately picked a few injuries up in one of them, which was Afghanistan. I've got two girls that I wanted to see grow up, so twelve years I've pretty much decided by then that I've done my bit for the country, and time to let someone else have their time.

JR: And family's a very strong pull, isn't it?

Leon: Yeah.

JR: And as long as I've known you, you've been a family man.

Leon: Yeah.

JR: I've never known you otherwise, and like the rest of us, all you want to do is get on with your life. It's not that you are some kind of animal that just wants to go around shooting people. It's a million miles from reality, isn't it? It's just where we are.

Leon: Right.

JR: So the day comes. You leave the army. Yeah. You go home. You've got your wish.

You're with your partner, I assume.

Leon: Yeah.

JR: You're with your two daughters.

Life ought to be sweet.

Leon: Ought to be, yes.

JR: And was it?

Leon: No.

JR: Okay. So let's take that forward then. If life wasn't sweet, what was the main problem?

Leon: I'd say my mental health.

JR: The longer I left it unresolved, the worse it got.

Leon: Yeah. I started drinking, going out every weekend, spending money basically.

I'm a big person for burying my head in the sand and not facing my issues rather than asking them. And all that does is build up like a volcano and then you erupt and head rest over here.

JR: And let's be fair about it, Leon. You're not alone. Many people will do this.

Leon: I'm the veterans rep in prison at the moment, and there's 15 ex-squaddies in here at the minute.

JR: And we're men, aren't we? We tend to not think about that.

Leon: Oh no, we can carry on. That's the problem. And we can't. And the sooner we learn that we can't and do something about it, the better.

JR: So drink was a problem in your life.

Leon: Basically, I was using drink to mask the problem of getting shit-faced.

JR: But were you also working at the time?

Leon: I was, yeah.

JR: Okay, as an electrician?

Leon: Electrician, yeah.

JR: So money was coming in, money was going out, and you were able to see your daughters?

Leon: Yeah.

JR: So that was good.

Leon: Yeah. They were in school, everything was regular. Life was sweet.

JR: But every now and again, you drank too much. And the result was?

Leon: Bar fights, being arrested, ended up in prison.

JR: You see, to somebody like me that, I don't wish to sound holier than thou, but somebody like me that's not been in prison other than with the guys I'm in with now, it's a very strange place to be. So I'm imagining I'm you, I'm out on a Friday night, I've had too much to drink, somebody's threatened me, I've punched them in the face, police have come along, taken me off to the local nick, and just locked me up for the night.

When I wake up in the morning, what's the reality?

Leon: Quite strange for me, see, when I lose my temper with my condition and the amount I've drunk. So basically, I see red, don't remember half the stuff that I've done until I woke up the next day. And it became a bit of a running joke at my local police station, where I'd get up, and the custody sergeant would say to me, do you even remember what you're here for, **Leon**? Because when you come in, you know, it wasn't the same you.

No. I've got a relationship with the sergeant there now, where I've been in that many times, he knows me by face, by name, by everything. So the sober me that he knows, he likes.

The drunken me that comes in, not so much. And he's often said the difference between the drunk you and the sober you is like massive. So the sober you is a nice person, I can't even see why you're in prison, but the drunk you is absolute nightmare.

JR: Well, the honesty is that when we first met all those months ago, you told me this. Yeah. You said, John, you wouldn't want to know me if I was drunk. And I've never seen you like that. So I've never had the problem.

Leon: No, that's it. So obviously, the more and more I've been in prison, the more I've had to sit and think of this. Obviously, something's got to give.

I can't keep coming here. I can't keep doing this. I've got kids to look after. Someone's got to change. And the reality is "more drunken" is the thing that's got to change.

JR: That's right. We do our little bit to help you.

Leon: Yes you do.

I'm lucky at the minute to have people that have been through that. I've got a good friend sitting next to me who's been through this, been through the prison life and was able to give me good advice on how to stop this. I suppose the danger of going out on a Friday night and getting drunk and finishing, waking up in the police cell the next morning, you could have done some serious harm and not even known it.

JR: So you might have thought, oh, I'll punch him on the nose. But actually, he's died of haemorrhage or something. And you're on a murder charge when, you know, I have never, ever perceived you as a dangerous person.

But you are when you've had a drink.

Leon: So I'm a trained soldier. I'm trained to kill.

Yeah. So I'm drunk and I'm not in control of my own skill set.

JR: And you're not alone, are you?

Leon: No.

JR: People coming out of the army, many of them will be in a similar position.

Leon: Yeah. Well, the thing is, when we go out, I don't look for the fights. I don't actively try and get it on. But if they happen, my training instinct is to fight back. That's why I get through straight through it.

And I still have that mentality. It's very hard once you've been a soldier to turn that mentality off because we're trying to just react and, you know, do things on instinct rather than stop and think about it. You stop and think about it, you're already dead.

Yeah. So it's very hard to get out of that way of life, out of that being a soldier.

See, when the creators, if you look throughout all the training, they want to show you what you're doing, the problem is you haven't got an off switch and it challenges you for life. There's no changing back from who you are.

JR: Of course not.

Leon: That's the hardest thing. So the only thing that you can do to mitigate that is stop the thing that's causing the issues.

JR: Absolutely right. But it's easier said than done. You need help.

Leon: Yeah.

JR: And do we ask for it always? That's another problem, isn't it?

Leon: You know, we don't see, we know there's a problem, but we don't really know how to react against it. So the judge said, Les, you're going to jail.

JR: First thoughts when you went through the door here, wherever am I, I suppose?

Leon: No.

Being a soldier is a lot like a prison. It's a lot of being back at the regiment. It's a house full of blokes. Being told when to eat, when to shit, when to shower. It's kind of home from home. It regularises your life.

JR: And importantly, it stops you getting the drink that is the base of the problem. So as long as you're in here, in a way, it must feel safer.

Leon: I wouldn't say safer. It just feels like home from home to a soldier. The barracks are pretty much bizarre. They've got a handle on both sides of the doors. They're locked. It's not too far dissimilar from being at a barracks in England.

JR: Okay. So let's get on to our first meeting. Because I can clearly recall it because I was just starting in this prison as well. And I was running a poetry course, and in marches is Les with all his mates.

Leon: Yeah.

JR: And I think you openly admitted later on you only came because it was a day out of your pad.

Leon: I did indeed. I sat down and I still laugh to this day. And John starts rattling on about poetry and limericks. And let's have a cup of tea, shall we? And have a chat. And at the end of the day, Leon thinks, do you know what? This has been a good day.

JR: Indeed. We both enjoyed it.

Leon: Poetry is a bit of a girly thing to do, isn't it? But I'll look back and laugh at that because obviously with the counselling, they teach us to get stuff out of your head, try and write it on a piece of paper. Yeah. And that gets it from your head to the paper, screw it up, chuck it away.

So I basically incorporated that method of counselling with your method of writing and come up with my own way of dealing with my own problems in my head while I'm sat here myself. Excellent.

JR: And it works for you.

Leon: It's worked for me ever since. And I think it would work for a number of people.

JR: So what I found, my side of the story was that when we started receiving the poetry back that you'd written and you confided in me that the problem with PTSD was a simple problem. The drugs they put you on in prison to cope with the PTSD kept you awake at night. And so when you're awake at night, what did Leon do? He wrote lovely poetry.

And he wrote the loveliest poems that I've ever read. And in the end, we put them into a book. It was great. And so we became friends. And I don't think that's ever going to change, to be honest, because I think that the situation that develops out of it is mutual respect and trust. And that's where you need to get to.

Leon: Well, basically, I think you give me a way of, a different way of coping with my PTSD. Obviously, rather than let it go over my head, I'm getting it written down on paper. But I've also now got a way of structuring it on paper so it actually sounds like an art form.

And coupling both of them together takes more time than it does just to write it down out of your head. So by the time I've actually finished writing some of these poems, whether it be the love poems or written on my scenes, whether it be the ones that I had when I flashed back and just get it out on paper. Yeah, the time it took to write these things down.

I'd already started thinking about something else in my head because I'm doing something productive. And it helped get it really good. So I can use my salvation in prison.

JR: Well, I hope so. I hope it helps. And I hope it helps other people as well because I thoroughly enjoyed doing it.

And I think generally speaking, at the end of it all, the men seem to say, thank you, John. I enjoyed that. But if I analyse you a little bit, I'm not a psychiatrist, but if I analyse you a bit more, it's led into other art forms, hasn't it? So your drawings are fantastic.

Your poetry continues. Your stories that have been published now in a book available on Amazon. A success of this prison really, a project that has been running in here and you were a major part of it and that remains so now.

All of these things combined, coupled with this overwhelming desire to be a dad, a partner, a provider, earn enough money for you all to have a quality of life. It's all come out of this. So you build on things, don't you?

Leon: Yeah, well, I think there's two types of prisoners.

There's one that will sit here and dwell on what they've done, go back out and not learn their lesson. And I think you've got the types like me that don't like to just sit in a cell, like to keep themselves active, don't want to keep coming back here and do something about it.

JR: And you're in that group?

Leon: I'm a go-do person.

JR: So while you've been in here, I know I've just repeated what you do with your time, but another thing you do is SAFA, isn't it? Just run us through SAFA, why you do it and what you get out of it.

Leon: So basically my job in prison is to look after all the armed forces veterans that we've got in here. So I work very closely with one of the officers who is called the VICSO, Veterans in Custody Support Officer. Basically what I do for him is I've got a list of all the ex-soldiers in here and I'll go around and visit them.

I've got claim forms for SAFA to get them financial help in here if they need it. Most people that come into prison either can't get a job straight away or have nowhere to go when they get out of prison. So I can do forms to send off to SAFA.

We have them come in once a month to a veterans forum where we all get together, have a coffee, pretty much what we're doing now, chat about what we need, what's going wrong. What works and what doesn't. We have a few charities coming, we have SAFA, a company called Stepway and also Care After Combat.

Each of them, veterans support units, give a different level of support. So SAFA's mainly financial.

JR: Could you just remind me what SAFA stands for?

Leon: Soldiers, Sailors, Airmen, Families Association.

JR: Ah okay, because obviously I've heard of it but never knew what it stood for.

Leon: Yeah and it's a powerful help. It's one of the main armed forces charities that there is and God bless her before the Queen, she was the head of that charity for a number of years since it began.

JR: Okay and it works well.

Leon: It does.

JR: Would you say they're a major part of your mindset change?

Leon: Yeah it's nice to give back. I've learned ways through my counselling and my recovery on how to remap my brain if you will, think in a different way, look at the positives in these situations because I was very much a pessimist. I'd always look at the worst, not look at the ways to get around it, where now I'm looking at the positive in every situation. The glass half full, not the glass half empty.

JR: Well I've always been that kind of person but it's the way to be but I'm a little bit biased you know. So let's think forward, let's look to the future now, let's look to Mr L's future. So how much longer do you think you might be in here?

Leon: Hopefully a week.

JR: Okay so it's nearly over and you will be going home to a partner, two daughters, a mum and work, that's the next thing, get a job and will you be going back to your electrical skill?

Leon: Mainly yeah.

JR: Okay and I think that's going to provide a good income. The regime though, when you leave here will you need to go to an approved premises or you can go straight home?

Leon: So it's time served, so only time will tell.

All the good work that's happened in here has got to produce the goods at the end of the day. Yeah. Superb. How old are you now Mr L?

Leon: I'm 37.

JR: Okay so I'm 75. You've got many many years in front of you. I'd like to wish you all the very best for the future. I'm convinced you will be fine but you know that myself and people that I've introduced you to will always be at the end of a phone line. Yeah. So we'll help you.

The change in your attitude at first, when I first knew you, you wouldn't look at your drinking. I think you knew in the back of your mind but it was just admitting to yourself that that was an issue. So I've seen the change in you and it really gives me hope for you.

Because before, because I was the same opinion of you as you were that ex-servicemen will easily become institutionalised because they're used to regime, they're used to being turned down, so it would be quite easy for you to get into the habit of coming back. So it's really good to see the change in your attitude

Well, I think from your perspective as well, Leon, being honest with yourself is the only solution. I don't think there's another one there, you know? Everyone being honest with themselves is the only solution.

You've got a good support network to go out to. You're very fortunate a lot of people haven't got that. Well, if nobody else, you've got Ed and me, you can always just get on the phone.

Another thing that I missed out was the fact that last year you did some abseiling for charity.

It's a key element of doing your duty, doing your service and giving back to people. Let's weave into that as well. So Effie's Bubbles and the institutionalisation.

Leon: Yeah, make sure you get the name, man. Effie's Bubbles. Careful how you say it.

No, you're saying it, not me. Don't ask me for it because I'll fuck up. Fucking Bubbles. You do realise now you're going to get the shit ripped out of you because you were meant to do it.

JR: Yeah, I don't care. I don't care though, Leon.

Leon: I'm very thin-skinned. So yes, John, so I did do this abseiling for you because you got too scared and your arse fell out.

JR: That sounds perfect.

Chapter 3

Jake

Jake's story is one of ambition, resilience, and struggle. Having joined the military at a young age, he embraced a career that took him across Europe, excelling in his role and even reaching the GB development squad for the biathlon.

However, his transition back to civilian life was far from smooth. A relationship that started with love and hope soon revealed deeper complications, leading to personal battles with mental health, loneliness, and a toxic environment that spiralled into prison.

His story is one of searching—for purpose, for stability, and most importantly, for a way back to his son. This conversation delves into his experiences, the failures of the rehabilitation system, and his fight to rebuild a life where he can finally be the father he wants to be.

The Interview . . .

JR: Let's talk about your childhood, growing up. How old are you now?

Jake: I'm 28.

JR: And life at home was good?

Jake: Yeah, so it was fairly normal as a child growing up.

JR: Mum and dad?

Jake: Yeah, mum and dad were around. I've got one sister; she's six years older than me. Now that she's got four children of her own, I've got one of my own now.

So, we've all pretty much grown up and moved out of the nest. As is perfectly normal. It's what everybody does, isn't it? Time goes on and we all make the best of whatever life deals to us.

JR: And you went to school, left school, got yourself a job, did you?

Jake: Yeah, so once I started to leave school, I had a bit of a rocky time going through school. It wasn't really for me as a kid. As a young boy, you don't really have the right mindset or you're not really ready for it back then.

So, I joined the army. I wanted to get as far away from home as possible. So, I did six years in the military, went on through my training, and got posted overseas to Germany. So, I lived in Germany for four and a half years.

And then the last year and a half of my career, I ended up getting into the GB development squad for the biathlon. I got into the highest level of sports within the army. And then I was competing for a GB spot. I lived in Norway for about a year of my life. Austria for about 10 or 11 months. France a year. And yeah, Bavaria as well. And then all of my summer training was over at Nova Scotia.

JR: Do you look back on your army career with happy memories?

Jake: Well, yeah, so it was fairly happy.

JR: No regrets?

Jake: Well, you do have regrets in there. Making mistakes and learning.

JR: Yeah, but that happens in life, doesn't it?

Jake: Yeah, all through life. But other than that, it was a great career.

JR: And mum and dad were proud of you?

Jake: Yeah, they were very proud.

JR: And your sister, of course. So you decided to come out of the army. What made you make that decision?

Jake: Ironically, I ended up meeting my ex-wife at the time.

She ended up going through great difficulty with the health of her children. I was planning on getting married to her quite quickly, which was a stereotypical army thing to do. But back in the day, yeah, I tried getting her to fly us over to Germany with me because she fell pregnant with my son at the time.

So it all went up in the air. From there, I decided to move back to the UK to start off with. But once I did, I didn't really like it.

It was a new regiment. The people in there were quite different and I was in a new place compared to living overseas. Because living overseas, you're actually quite a tight-knit family over there.

You live there constantly. You go back to the UK in the army and everybody goes home on the weekends. So you don't really get to see people.

You don't really get to mingle as much as you should. It's just a completely different mindset, really. The word that comes into my mind is loneliness.

JR: Would you say that was a problem at the time?

Jake: Yeah, massively. Because me transferring to a new regiment, I had to meet new people, meet the new chain of command as well.

JR: Do they accept you?

Jake: No, not really.

They see you as an outsider. You're going from one regiment to another regiment. Because the army's got the mentality of, "We've got the best regiment," or "We've got the better this." And then it's always, "Oh, you've come from that regiment, so it's a bit different."

JR: So you travelled around quite a bit by the sounds of it. And then found yourself back in the UK. And really, if I'm reading it right, you've done that because your partner, the mother of your child, didn't want to move out of England.

Jake: No, because she had difficulties with her children in the end.

JR: Did she have children before she had your child?

Jake: Two of her children. She didn't actually have custody of them, so she applied for custody for them. That was the reason why I came back.

JR: That was a good reason, wasn't it? That she wouldn't want to leave England because of it. I knew I no doubt could understand that reason.

Jake: Yeah, but unfortunately, she didn't win custody of them. And then once my son was actually born as well, I realised why she didn't actually have custody of them. She struggled a lot to look after herself, so it was a big, massive strain to try and look after another child as well.

JR: Let's explore that a little bit. Why does she have trouble looking after the child? Is she in love with being pregnant and giving birth, but then loses interest? Or has she got a mental health problem?

Jake: She's got mental health problems.

JR: What's the story?

Jake: She comes from quite a rocky family herself. Her mum's actually an alcoholic. Her dad actually hung himself in prison. So she's had a bit of nasty stuff in her life anyway.

Yeah, so she hasn't had the best upbringing or a safeguarded upbringing compared to what I had.

Mine wasn't perfect, but from there, I could see the damage within her. I thought, I've done so well in my life up to now, I've made a big, massive change from what my childhood was compared to where I got to. I thought I could put what I had into her to help her get better.

JR: It must have come as quite a shock to realise that you couldn't.

Jake: Oh no, massively. It was probably one of the biggest downfalls of my life.

JR: Biggest disappointment you've ever had, I would think. So it ended up being a very toxic relationship in the end ?

Jake: Yes, it brought out a lot of mental health difficulties which I was undiagnosed with at the time, which was actually childhood related to myself.

So from there I was trying to look after myself which I know how to look after myself but I have to put in a lot of time to look after myself and I didn't have that time to commit. So then I got more and more ill over time and then it ended up breaking down and I actually ended up in prison the very first time.

JR: It sounds like a downward spiral that you haven't really got any control over.

Jake: No.

JR: A chance in life that just happened and I don't think you're alone. I think there are lots of people that have walked this path and whether there's a solution to it, there certainly isn't a quick solution is there? But what the actual solution would be, who knows because for whatever reason you finished up in prison and here you are. And by chance you and I met and I hope in some small way I helped you. Because that's what it's all about really. We talk about poetry and we talk about reading and we talk about chit chat really, don't we? But at the end of the day I try and form some kind of friendship with all of the students and we do that in a variety of ways.

Not least, simply chatting and listening. Did you not find too many people doing that in prison? Do they not listen to you?

Jake: I'm sort of massively in awe of both sides of the spectrum. You get people prisoner wise and officer wise that will go in one ear and go completely out the other ear.

It's a shame. The rehabilitation system within the UK is completely backwards compared to what you see overseas in a different country. So take Norway for example, I lived there for a year but their rehabilitation system actually takes three years to train an officer up.

They actually go into work straight away all of their money gets put into a pot when they get released they actually get funding for stuff so they get a business out of it or they get a house deposit, they actually get help and support properly.

JR: Some would argue that that would encourage crime so you can go in and learn how to run a business.

Jake: You wouldn't think of it that way because they delve in to what your problem is compared to the UK. They do a lot of things where they can say oh yeah we can help in this sector we can help to find work but the work that they actually find is work which a lot of people earn more money on benefits so it's a no brainer for a lot of people to stay on benefits or unemployed.

JR: Yeah if they just judge it financially without thinking about their mental health but I remember on the course you were struggling with your mental health and I'd like to explore if I may what the prison do to help you in that respect so the most obvious way they can help you of course is to get you on a drug regime that helps you and how did the prison go about doing that?

Jake: So when I actually first came into prison I was in a really dark place with everything that's gone on with the contact issues not being able to talk to my son and stuff so I was self-harming a lot. I ended up trying to hang myself in prison just before I met you. And then I ended up having more and more mental breakdowns.

So how I cope with things I take things out on myself a lot of the time instead of taking it out on other people. But I always do have the risk of taking it out on somebody else when there is an episode so on the actual courts they actually try and find out what sort of things they can do to help you minimise all of this.

They're meant to put in a safety reduction plan but a lot of the time they write it down but then it's great difficulty for them to actually follow it up and put it in place.

JR: Why is that?

Jake: It's just how the prison system works. A lot of different prisons, well I've been to three different prisons so I can't talk of a wide variety, but compared to the other two that I've been to this one it's actually been one of the slowest processes of the prison system that I've ever been in.

So they don't do the kiosks in here they don't do things with a computer so the process is a lot slower you go to a different prison everything's on a kiosk.

JR: What do you mean by a kiosk?

Jake: So it's got the computer system within the prison so everything's done on General Ops here which is a paper app a lot of the times it will go missing for example, or you wouldn't get a response in a set amount of time. You're actually meant to get a response in five days and sometimes you're waiting up to three weeks for a response or you don't even get a response.

JR: But if things are done on the computer system you'll do it and you'll get a response within three days for example and I suppose if you're mentally perhaps depressed or anxious you know, you want things to come right straight away, don't you?

Jake: Yeah, it needs to get prioritised.

Because in regards to my mental health as well as I say, our mental health can help support you we can get you to the doctor or the psychiatrist within the prison and they can actually medicate you.

I should actually be on quetiapine, which is an antipsychotic and over the five months I've been in the prison now I've actually been asking for my medication to be approved. Again it's been on my doctor's record that I took it previously and the psychiatrist hasn't once consulted me to see me in person, they've just took mental health feedback from on my app reports.

When I've been sitting on my app reviews for five minutes and next thing you know they say oh yeah, we'll talk to the psychiatrist, we'll put it over the psychiatrist goes, oh no he doesn't need the medication, we declined his medication all he needs is emotional support.

So I was just going to say I've shown no signs of psychotic episodes I've self-harmed I've tried killing myself I've ended up even assaulting officers in prison as well, which is very unprofessional, but it was me in a heightened state. I had a mental breakdown so I pushed past a couple of officers and now I've got a mountain on top of my head because I'm looking at extra charges now. They haven't reviewed the CCTV to see that I haven't done what they've said in there as well so it's quite disheartening you're trying to be truthful and as open as possible to help and support but no-one wants to say we'll help them.

In their sector it's quite disheartening but I've got into the stage now where I'm getting completely numb to it all.

JR: OK, well I'm not in any position to comment on that, and I won't because I've not experienced it and obviously, I'm not qualified to do that either so there we are. I remember seeing your arms you've got some marks on your arms that I'm looking at now and I know what you're doing I have the greatest difficulty, as I think many, many people on the outside will have in understanding why would somebody do that? Does it not hurt? and I know that I've asked you in the past, does it not hurt? and you say, well a lot of the time it doesn't, no but if you were a prison officer discovering a man sat in his cell self-harming it would be quite upsetting for the prison officer because their only human. You might not be their favourite person, but they are there for you and me really.

So what relief do you get from self-harming? How does it help?

Jake: It's a coping mechanism when I'm having my actual episodes it's a mixture of using it as a coping mechanism to relieve all the stress but then when I do it as well at the same time, I'm not doing it for attention, I'm not doing it for a release but I'm trying to do it to end my life at the same time as well.

But it's a really complex thing within my own mind because one of my biggest fears is death so I'm putting myself back into a feared state when I'm having a mental breakdown as it is anyway, but then I don't care about that fear at the time so it's a strange one.

JR: We could summarise this couldn't we, to say that the way you are in prison, in the way you deal with other people, whether they're prison officers or fellow inmates, is entirely down to your mental health, and your mental health is not what it should be. But what are the chances of getting it the way it should be in this prison or indeed any other prison I honestly don't know ?

Jake: It's very, very slim because when I was in the army for example, I was at my best I was at my peak, I was doing fitness three times a day, which I believe helps your mental health, because it releases all your endorphins in your body and gives you a better health, the food's a lot better, so you can actually eat structured foods, more healthy foods which you don't really get in prison so it's a lot of carb overloading in prison and that isn't going to help people's mindset either and then the lock-up as well.

Like, there's prisons still doing 23-hour lock-up a day so if you cage an animal for 23 hours a day, what's it going to do? Bite you. It's going to bite back eventually.

JR: Yeah, of course it is, of course it is.

But the fact that you're able to talk to me about it what can we learn from that? I would hope a lesson for me anyway, is that you are an approachable kind of guy, and I'm certainly a pair of ears to listen, I've every sympathy with your situation and I've had that advantage of working with you in a classroom and we both enjoyed the experience so, again it talks about a downward spiral in that, if you do something you shouldn't, and you know you shouldn't you know you shouldn't self-harm, you know you shouldn't hit a prison officer, you know you shouldn't whatever, it's not that you don't know it, it's just that you're driven to the frustration of doing things without thinking and that's the be all and end all of it really. What do you think this prison or indeed any prison, could do to help you at this stage of your life?

Jake: A lot of it is getting them trained properly to listen, so if they actually listen to people and prisoners properly actually understand the problems and actually help to try and follow up on it it's going to help a prisoner tenfold compared to what they actually do, because a lot of the time they'll pay lip service to things, like pretend that, oh yeah we'll take it and we'll follow it up.

JR: And would this person be highly trained or would they be somebody like me that just as I do, sit and chat with you?

Jake: Well a lot of the time you could just sit and chat and it helps people a lot more.

JR: You've said to me more than once on leaving the room, thank you John, and all I've done is sat and chatted I'm not a highly trained psychiatrist or anything Just treating somebody like a human is completely different than treating them like they mean absolutely nothing I've spoken to many people and as you know, one of the first things I say to people when first we meet, the crime is irrelevant I'm not the slightest bit interested in your crime what I'm interested in talking to you about is you as a person. I will trust and respect you if you return that, and in every kind of dealing that I've had with you you've done that for me, you've never ever offended me or upset me or threatened me or done me any harm.

In return I haven't ever done that to you, and never would but it's a difficult thing in a large organisation to get everybody caring in the same way because caring is a special thing isn't it ? And that leads me on to your little boy just remind me what we did for you and your little boy while we were together did we write a poem about him ?

Jake: Yeah, so I was writing poems so I was involved in all of my poems so I've got quite a few different dark poems but then I've got quite nice ones as well.

JR: I remember you gave me seven all in one day !

So you like writing poetry, did I get them typed out for you at the time ?

Jake: Yeah you did, so I've got them all in my cell.

JR: And do they help you ?

Jake: Yeah they do.

JR: Do you find comfort in them ?

Jake: Yeah massively, so when I'm struggling at times and I can actually focus to put pen to paper and get emotions out, it helps massively.

JR: Well you've got prison to thank for that because whatever else they do wrong, nevertheless they pay me to come in and do that and that's been a help to you so it's a matter really I suppose of how much good balances how much bad things that don't really help things that make the matters worse if they are greatly outnumbered by the things that are acts of kindness, acts of help. I know you've got friends on the wing that you can sit and talk to indeed one of them is sitting here with us now listening to all this, I know he helps you as much as he can, and he will and I think there will be a camaraderie won't there amongst people living in a prison and I hate the word prisoner because whilst I accept that you are a prisoner, in my world you're a resident of here and living here at the moment and it's a bit of a nuance and a play on words but nevertheless I think it's part of the picture of showing you that there are lots of people like me that care.

So where are we with your little boy then you're able to write to him?

Jake: Well ironically social services confirmed that I could do letterbox contact.

JR: Which means you can write to him ?

Jake: Yeah, I can write to him but I've ended up making loads of nice things to send over to him.

JR: Does he live locally?

Jake: Well I know that he's going to be over Stratford sort of area.

JR: Not far then, it's going to be about half an hour for him and will he be living with his mum?

Jake: I know he's in foster care currently.

JR: OK so mum is not in a position to look after him so your mission then in your head is to get out and get with him as soon as you can or as soon as you'll be allowed to. So you can write to him but how old now is he? 4? 5?

OK, he can write to you in pictures he can draw things and send it in if the foster carer posts it. Yeah but then social will be holding what from him to you or from you to him? I would say that's important to do because when all this comes to an end and it surely will you will be able to say to him I did my best I might not have been the perfect dad but I did as much as I possibly could to keep the relationship right and to keep it in a way that you'll love me, respect me, trust me as we both get older together

Jake: Yeah I would never give up on him.

JR: No I can see that so what's the plan then? when you leave here I've no desire to know how long that will be but whenever it is what's the plan? Have you got a trade or a skill that you can make a living at?

Jake: I'm working in construction now currently, just before I come in I was working on the HS2 project so I was doing a lot of machines working with the piloting crew building all the rail line, all the footings and foundations the railway to nowhere.

JR: The railway that's going to cost the country about 80 billion and they're only going to make a profit back in about 100 years so that's a whole new debate but I share your thoughts on HS2 but from your perspective if it's a potential employer, which it is and I believe the wages are quite good, then that's the plan isn't it? Because number one if you want a stable family background to allow your son to come back in your life you'll need somewhere to bring him to somewhere safe, somewhere that the social can say he's not going to come to any harm and actually, he would benefit you as much as you would benefit him because if you think about it there are many old people out there that have a pet dog or a pet cat, just for the company.

You're a younger man you don't need pets, if you've got your little boy and you can look after him then that will mean your life's complete, whether there's a lady in your life or not, remains to be seen and wouldn't it be lovely I don't know how possible it is but wouldn't it be lovely if the little boy's mum also found her feet and came to live with you and you were back as a family. Maybe that will never happen but it will never happen ever if you haven't got a plan, so there has to be a plan.

At some point I'd like to think there are lots of things in this prison that are done to help people, to take their brain away from where it is now, because everything that you're going through is mentally driven isn't it so the self-harming, the stress, the anxiety all the other mental health problems that you've got if you could overcome the mental health problems you would be in a much better place.

And if you then get out of here, I mean, with all respect to criminals of this land you don't, in my world, fit the image of one that I would think, goodness look at this man, he's something terrible you don't, you look a man where the system is winning at the moment. Now, what about your mum and dad, are they still around

Jake: Yeah, so my mum and dad are still around.

JR: Do they have access to the little boy ?

Jake: Well, no, so apparently my mum was in a breach of the contacts, even though social services told her, didn't tell us any information, that my son wasn't allowed to talk to me over the phone. He was going to see my mum once a month but the rest of my family put a block in place saying that my mum's breached and he wasn't meant to be talking to me but at no point did they turn around and say he's not allowed to talk to his dad so it was a bit of a sticky situation, so they've blocked all contact with me, blocked all contact with my mum and it's been about four months, since yeah, about four months

JR: So this situation impacts you, but it impacts your mum and dad as well, I'm a grandfather myself, to be cut off from my grandchildren would be one of the most painful things you could do to me because I don't want to be cut off, I might not see them every day but I do see them and a major part of my life, so your mum and dad, if they can't see your little boy, and actually if you think about it, your mum can be a surrogate mother to the little boy, if his mum is not around, your mum can help out can't she?

Jake: Yeah massively, my son is always going, nanny can I stay over, can I stay with you can I stay with you because that's what they like doing isn't it? it's just heartbreaking that we're in such a sticky situation with the social services.

JR: And that doesn't help your mental health, does it?

Jake: No, but if social actually worked for me properly and they'd actually realise that I'm a damn good father that they've got no concerns all of my contact reports they can't find one fault against me.

JR: Well you're never going to hurt him, are you?

Jake: No, so I feed him healthy food, I've got good boundaries, he listens to me but everything I've ever done with social services has never been good enough and they've always dropped something on me saying oh he hasn't done this or we feel that this is it.

JR: It's all opinionated, so they're always putting negative opinions on you but they're not here to defend themselves but if I might put in a word for them they are in a difficult position aren't they? they are massively overworked they're underfunded and they're doing the best they can within the limitations of what they've got in the same way that the prison services and the police services and the national health services, all of our country is in the hands of these big organisations and I think there are some nasty people in all of them but they're very few and far between so I would think in the case of your little boy, if truth were spoken they're doing the best they can within their limitations but that's not the solution for you is it?

The solution for you is to be back with your son, so I think the only way forward is to concentrate on what you're doing here in prison, helping yourself as much as possible because you're the one that's got the most to gain from taking part in anything and in respect of the courses available I would have loved you to have come back onto my course after the incident with the prison officer, it wouldn't have in any way affected me but I can see from the prison officer's point of view, this is a difficult situation, we don't want to reward somebody, they may see a training course as a reward a day out your pad when actually he's a naughty boy so it's that old balancing act again isn't it?

Jake: Yeah, well I already did my punishment, so I already did the 11 days in segregation and the 28-day basic regime so I already completed that punishment so I was actually still on the list to come over to you.

JR: Don't misunderstand me I'm not defending them.

Jake: No, not at all I would love to come back onto it because I was only half way through the course. But there we are so I can see in my mind there isn't a clear path to your solutions on the outside however, I'm also the eternal optimist, I also think that things happen for a reason, certainly in my life they always have and in your life, it's going to be the same as it will with everybody on this planet.

JR: I think the only comment I would make it's not really advice, is do what you're doing, keep your head down you know, make the best of a bad job really and in the back of your mind always keep the thought that sooner or later you're going to be with your boy again and when you are your mental health will improve dramatically, you can settle back onto your job of work mum can maybe help out with the babysitting who knows what might happen with a female in your life.

Chapter 5

Lincoln

Prison is a world few of us will ever experience, yet for those who do, the reality is stark, isolating, and often life-altering. Today's conversation is with Lincoln, a man who, by most definitions, had it all—a thriving business, a strong work ethic, and a structured life built on ambition and hard work. But, as is often the case, life can take unexpected turns, and he now finds himself navigating an entirely different system—one where routine is imposed, personal freedom is restricted, and the future is uncertain.

Unlike the dramatic arrests we see in films, Lincoln's entry into the justice system was different. He voluntarily walked into a police station, believing the truth would protect him. Now, awaiting trial on remand, he faces a reality few could comprehend. The transition from boardrooms to prison cells is as jarring as it is profound, and through this conversation, we explore the emotional toll, the loss of autonomy, and the unexpected moments of humanity found behind bars.

We discuss his first impressions of prison life, the impact on his family, and the psychological weight of incarceration. He speaks with raw honesty about the struggle to adapt, the moments of despair, and the lifelines—however small—that have helped him cope. This is not just a story about imprisonment; it's about resilience, self-reflection, and the search for purpose in the most challenging of circumstances.

As we begin, I ask him about the first moments of walking through the prison doors, a moment that marks the start of an experience that will change him forever.

The Interview . . .

JR: Tell me Lincoln, how much of a shock was it when you first came through the door?

Lincoln: Well, the whole experience from waiting to hear what the judge thinks and being put on remand and not being allowed to go home, right through to the journey here, you know, the van journey, walking through the gates, It's alien. I don't care who you are, it's extraordinary, it's a terrifying feeling as well. The unknown, with anything, is always difficult. Coming through the gates, particularly in walking in, it's intimidating and, yeah, I suppose I was very fearful.

JR: Many people will imagine it begins with "the knock", but in your case it did not, tell me all about that fateful day please.

Lincoln: Well, it actually wasn't with me, my experience was different and I actually went to the police with my lawyers. But yeah, you know, I'm on remand so I'm waiting for a trial date. That is, I suppose, different from when you're actually sentenced.

JR: Yeah, because people on the outside, in the majority of cases, won't have experienced what happens when you get arrested. So what happened to you was, you went into the police station and finished up on remand.

Lincoln: Yeah, yeah, essentially.

JR: Innocent or guilty ? Only you will know, but you have to decide what you are going to plea, and how easy is that ? And what a shock to the system because at the moment you're an innocent man.

Lincoln: Well, I will always claim that I'm innocent and I will always, to the day I die, but that's really, you know, that's just one of those things, isn't it? Yeah, that's the way the system works. I think it's a very complicated system and, yeah, it's probably a subject we stay clear of in here.

JR: Well, I'm trying to imagine the day you walk into the prison, the doors bang behind you, they show you where you're going to sleep that night. It's a relatively bare cell. There might be somebody else in it, there might not. At the most there's going to be two of you in there. It's dark, it's nighttime. You've maybe been given a simple meal to last you till the morning. It must be surely the loneliest place on earth ?

Lincoln: I think the first week particularly, and that first night as well, there wasn't any food when I arrived anyway because I arrived late. So I hadn't eaten since the morning, I think. And, yeah, when that door closes behind you and you're simply left with a very basic bed, a toilet and a sink all in one room, which is the sort of size of an en-suite in a nice hotel, so it's like living in a bathroom.

JR: At this moment you were alone. No way of contacting your family, hungry, completely confused, lonely, upset, the range of emotions must be overwhelming.

Lincoln: Yes. there's nothing there, and that first week's particularly difficult because you don't have access to your family. And because I'd never been in prison before, it was quite a steep learning curve trying to work out, well, how do I put my phone numbers on the list so I can actually call out, things like that. So for the first week I didn't actually speak to my wife or any family or friends, and so I did feel hugely isolated. I had no idea whether my wife had left me or was still with me.

JR: It must have been very difficult, so many thoughts running wild in your mind, how long did that feeling last ?

Lincoln: You know, five or six days later or a week later, I found out she was massively behind me and has been and will be always. But, yeah, that first week is a huge challenge. I can't explain to anybody.

JR: Yeah, I don't think anybody on the outside can imagine what it must feel like because unless you've done it, as you quite rightly say, it was all news to you, you didn't know how to perform, you know, but the simple things in life, like picking up a phone. In this day and age, everybody has a mobile phone. I'm sure you had one before you came in here. And if you wanted to make a phone call, if you wanted to talk to anybody, particularly your wife, you just picked the phone up and dialled it.

Lincoln: You know, the good thing is now I've got access to a phone. I have a phone in my room. I've got certain numbers I am able to ring. The difficulty is I have only got a maximum of two hours I can use on a day. And for me, I'm trying to run businesses in here still and have calls with my various management directors to make sure things are carrying on. It's not easy.

JR: As I said previously, before this happened you built a hugely successful business, and so how do they continue to trade, or do they continue to trade ? I had apportioned so much of my time and energy, a minimum of 12 hours a day, 7 days a week, that was my working day. From the moment I got up in the morning until I got home, I was working. Ultimately, I never really switched off mentally. That was a big mistake and that caused me massive emotional and mental stress over the years. And probably just resulted in the fact that I had been put into this vulnerable position and why I've ended up in here.

The challenging times with COVID, then followed by this, we haven't really bounced back after COVID. So some of my businesses have struggled massively, some we've had to shut down, we've had to let quite a few members of the team go. But yeah, the restrictions of the telephone make it even more challenging. But I do have that phone in the room, which is a lifeline to the outside world and keeps me sane.

JR: Some on the outside would argue that you shouldn't even have that phone. They would say that, you know, prison is a place of punishment, but again, because you're on remand, what are you being punished for at the moment?

Lincoln: Well, I suppose people don't really understand, do they? So for example, I'm in here and I've got to try and work with my lawyers and my family and people who are helping me with my case. So of course you need contact. How are you supposed to contact people? And I also think it's convenient for the prison. I think it's common sense. It makes their life and the officer's life easier, just having something like that, keeping the prisoners contained in their rooms and keeping them occupied.

JR: I've been coming to prison longer than you have and I know that pre-COVID it was different, very different. And it seems to me that what COVID has done is completely overhauled the system to the point where we are today. But I come back to my point in the first place, you know, it is extremely lonely. Not only the first night you're here, but they're on after because how do you know who your friends are?

Lincoln: Well, you don't. And that's another interesting thing. I was lucky in some ways. I went to a good school, got a scholarship as a kid and that paid for me to go to a musical school. So I was used to living around lots of male people. And so coming in here is quite similar. I would say the food's quite similar. And there are always types of people that you'll get on with and there will be types that you won't. And so people gravitate and you find like-minded souls and you just get by. One of the difficult things is the transition. You watch people that you develop a relationship with and friendship. You watch them go. So yesterday somebody went who's been a good friend. And today another one looks like they're going, they're in court. So yeah, that's tricky. Just watching people come and go and I still remain here, being stuck here.

JR: I'll take you back to your journey from the court to the prison. First experience, I've never been in one of these, used to be called black maria's, but I understand white now. What fears were going through your mind on that journey?

Lincoln: I suppose it's the unknown and would I ever see my wife again? Would I ever see my children again? Or when? And where am I going? What's it going to be like? Those types of things. But these are things that are experiences and they shape you and what doesn't kill you makes you stronger. And I think this whole experience of being in here, I'll come out of here a better person. Regardless of the fact that I believe I'm innocent, well I know I am innocent, but that's by the by. I will still come out of here a better person because I'm using my time in here to reflect.

JR: Looking back over your life, what could you have done better ?

Lincoln: There are many things that I could have always done better. I think we can all say that. I am reading more, I'm helping people learn to read English and I help people with various different problems. Reading their legal letters and things like that, helping them communicate with families when they run out of credit. There's all sorts of things that you can actually do to help people and that gives you a sense of satisfaction in itself. I think I've found since I've been coming into prison that not all the men in here are bad.

JR: That's the biggest lesson I've learned and the vast majority are not bad. I'd agree with that. I would say the vast majority obviously, whether good or bad, have made some bad decisions.

Lincoln: But great people and nice people and fantastic people can make bad decisions. I know a lot of people on the outside or in the real world who've made some bad decisions and they probably would be more likely to be the type of person you'd expect in here. So it's not everybody gets caught and I'm surrounded by people who probably regret their way, but it is also a way of life for some people. And you see people leaving and then bizarrely coming back as short a time as three days later.

JR: I've seen that myself. And I think the reason for it is because they feel safer in here than they are on the outside.

Lincoln: Well there's a camaraderie in here. You've got a roof over your head, you've got food. I would argue that some of the people in here will have more friends than if they were living on a park bench outside and trying to make ends meet. There's a lot of disadvantaged people that end up in these types of places.

People who have had appalling upbringings and not the type of opportunities that I think I've been lucky enough to have. And it's difficult for people to see a future sometimes when they're out. There are courses in here. I've done some. I'm lucky I can read and I can do maths, but I still read the papers and I'm still learning in here. But not everybody sees that as the right way to go and I think more work needs to be done. But I think more people could do the education courses.

JR: I noticed from your t-shirt that you're a Shannon Trust mentor. So tell me a bit about Shannon Trust and why you want to get involved with that.

Lincoln: Well, that's a small charity and that's to do with teaching people how to read and write. My wife spent most of her time with the children doing the education, helping them with their education.

While I was stereotypically working stupid hours every day, I regret that now massively. I see how much fun it is and how much will a sense of satisfaction I get from teaching people and seeing them learn. I've got people here who couldn't read their canteen sheet, so had no idea how to order things. They couldn't read basic letters that were coming in from friends and family or write back to them. And I'm now seeing particularly one of those that I'm working with. His reading is about confidence and his confidence level has gone through the roof. It's incredible to see what he can now do.

JR: It's not only incredible to see what he can do, but also to see what it's doing for you because it's giving you such a purpose in life and such a degree of satisfaction in seeing what you're achieving with him that you're gaining out of it as well.

Lincoln: Well 100% and it's good use of the prison's time for me. They're putting me to work if you like and that keeps me out of the cell. So originally when I came in here, I was 23 hours a day in the cell. If I was lucky, I mean sometimes you'd be slightly less than that. And when it is so long you do count every minute. But once you get a job and so the Shannon Trust has empowered me to go and help others. But at the same time, I'm out of my cell significantly less and I'm using that time to benefit others. It's a win-win for the prison, it's a win-win for the people I'm helping and I'm also getting huge satisfaction out of it.

JR: I know exactly what you mean because I remember talking to you on one of your first days on the wing I don't know how long when I basically came up and said, Hello, you alright? And that's all it took. And you looked at me and I could tell from your eyes that you weren't alright. And then I said do you want to come and do a bit of poetry and you did. And what would you say the poetry did for you?

Lincoln: Well, I'm a creative always have been and I don't think it's so much the poetry but it was the fact that somebody actually asked me am I okay? It'd been the first time in probably three months and I was pretty suicidal. I think that's the issue is being locked up 23 hours a day. Eventually your life eats away, it becomes a spiral and you're unable to develop a relationship with the officers and when I say a relationship just rapport. So to get out of that, to get an actual job becomes very, very hard. Eventually thanks to one of the staff members in here she replied to me and put me onto the list of the Shannon Trust and that was the game changer really. And I went from being somebody who I probably would have committed suicide. I'd worked out how I was going to do it.

JR: I'd like to talk to you about suicide if I may because I've had people in my life that have succeeded at committing suicide, they've died. And every single time it happens I think I wish I had known I could have helped them not do that and you're one of the few people I've ever spoken to that have said "I felt suicidal but nothing happened" because your way through it was that somebody helped you. And it was only a little thing that they did.

Lincoln: Yeah, but it was a little thing to you but it made a huge difference to me and the poetry course connected me with the member of staff who then got me on the Shannon Trust eventually. But yeah, I don't think I'd be here. I think I'd sort of made peace with my maker and worked out with my family and girls were probably better off without me. Obviously, it wasn't true but it was the way your mind was working and it was an indication of the mental anguish you were going through. Yeah, I mean I still have doubts with the pressure that my family are under. I still have doubts that, you know, am I a millstone around their neck but they're the ones, they come and see me three times a week because I'm allowed two more visits which is a blessing and my wife comes three times a week on her own on a Wednesday and then with different kids on different days on the Monday and the Saturday and that's again that's the oxygen that keeps me going.

JR: I would say that your survival is down to one word really and it's family. Yeah, I'm going to say that. Because you know we all need a family of kind. My friend calls it his tribe. If you have your colleagues, friends, call them what you will. If you've got people that you enjoy conversing with, you enjoy relating to, you share thoughts about life and whatever else is happening in the world. I think it's such a tremendous strength and I often wonder whether people with a mental health that may be in prison is controlled by drugs could actually be controlled by having a friendship with somebody.

Lincoln: Yeah, I think that's very true. And I also think structure, structure is really important as well knowing you have things to look forward to and so with a family I know I ring my little ones to say goodnight every night at the same time, although it seems to be getting later and later and they're always pushing the boundaries. But that's because that's what kids do.

JR: No it's lovely. Those are things you obviously miss enormously and you probably don't appreciate the things that you have and take for granted when you're on the outside.

Lincoln: But yeah that structure helps me get through the week as well having things to look forward to. The visits, I have two gym sessions a week I had three but one clashes with the visit and then every month I'm able to do a 5k run and then in my exercise period I run every day no matter what so I try and do about 40 kilometres, over 40 kilometres running a month.

JR: I'd like to say me too but it would be a lie.

Lincoln: I mean it's not that much when you think about it it's only just over a kilometre a day but some days I'll do three some days I'll do five and some days I'll just do everything.

JR: It's a little bit frustrating for you just run running in a circle out in the yard.

Lincoln: But you know what the moment they shout out exercise I've trained myself I just go downstairs and that's what I do so if there's an opportunity there and the officers laugh at me because especially if it's pouring with rain I take great pleasure in it just that feeling of we've just been connected to nature and it's lovely. And we're lucky here because we've got good exercise facilities. We do, it'd be great to have it where you could go to the gym a little bit more often I think that's probably a common theme you hear from people. But you know the gym staff are great and so I look forward to it.

JR: And this morning we've had the pleasure of hearing through the open window they've had a family fun day there on the exercise area. That's a wonderful gesture because I think for more people if you can maintain that family tie then you're halfway to surviving.

Lincoln: Yeah it is but it's hard for me because I have a family and I'm not able to do the family day. I'm on a VP wing and it's not accessible to me and that's one of those things. Yeah it doesn't work. Well they've said they're going to try and put one together but it's like everything takes time. I think also the situation in the criminal justice system at the moment with increasing numbers of prisoners.

JR: I like to use the word "residents" but most people are known as prisoners and they have a decreasing number of staff to look after them.

An economic problem.

Lincoln: I think there is difficulty in supplying what they would love to supply. It's frustrating for me because obviously I see this as a business from the inside. If you own a hotel the best way to see the business is go and book yourself in and see how the customer sees it. So I'm looking at this now as a prison. I think when I'm out I might actually look to build prisons or certainly get involved with the prison system somehow and I see the huge amount of money and time and resources could be saved by very simple software which would allow the officers to do the things that they're good at being supportive and helping people through the day.

We are lucky you know particularly on this wing. I know we've got some great officers. They are supportive individuals and you can tell the difference between it's a happy wing because people just get things done.

JR: As you know you and I have just spent the last 12 weeks talking about reading one day a week for 12 weeks and I've thoroughly enjoyed your company during that course but actually what the reading course is about it's about relating to people and relating to the trust and respect between the two and essentially that's what you're alluding to isn't it when you talk about the good prison officers. And I think in any group of employees or just general population if you like there's going to be good and bad. They're not all going to be absolutely perfect. Or varying degrees of good. But what would you say is your ideal prison officer? What does he or she look like?

Lincoln: I think the single most important thing would be the supportive gene but that's what I've always looked for in business anyway because a supportive person will go out of their way to make things happen. And that doesn't mean that a supportive person has to be a pushover far from it. I would say the officers here that are supportive are probably the strongest and the toughest but they're fair. So being fair and egalitarian and supportive I think they are key traits, but I think those traits help you in any area of life. So if you can develop those as people then you'll be successful as a prison officer, as a dad, as a mum, as a business person or whether you work in a shop or whatever you do.

JR: As you know I'm now 75 years of age and I find that as I've got older I've more and more understood that people respond to kindness and I suppose I'd like to think I'm as kind now as I'm ever going to be and having spent many hours with you discussing all these things I know that you're of the same frame of mind.

Lincoln: It's the kindness that touches you that you don't expect so I went through a bail hearing yesterday and didn't get it on the technicality and my wife was obviously devastated and I told myself I wouldn't get excited but obviously I was massively excited even without realising it. I came back to the wing and the SO (Senior Officer) here, he just looked at me and said, (he already knew that I hadn't got it and that I would be massively disappointed) look if you need any money on your phone credit, emergency phone credit, just let me know. I didn't but what a great guy and that type of character you could put in any business and he would be successful. And it's only a small thing isn't it, but It's colossal.

Especially when you're in a place like this where you are feeling vulnerable at times and you are feeling uncared for and obviously you're going to be feeling unloved but I'm lucky because on the outside I've got this massive support. But there are lots of people in here that don't have that so I think it's up to us as prisoners to make sure we look after the fellow comrades in the block.

JR: I think so and I think that's where a training course comes in as well because you all gel together don't you? You get to know other people in a different way and those that do need a bit of help, and I've seen you do this, get the help just because they're there and they're asking and it's obvious how easy it is to help.

JR: You say you have learned lessons in prison. What lessons will you take from prison that you're building to your business life?

Lincoln: Probably less so for my business although there must be some and making sure that I'm a better listener and a better, more supportive although I'd like to think I was pretty good at those sorts of things, but I think more in my family life. I had a portion of my time and energy, a minimum of 12 hours a day, 7 days a week which I didn't even bat an eyelid and that was my working day. From the moment I got up in the morning to the moment I went to bed. Even after I got home I was still doing things. So there's a minimum of 12 hours a day, that's too long and yes I had breaks within that I would have gone to the gym but ultimately I never really switched off mentally. That was a big mistake and that's caused me massive emotional and mental stress over the years and probably has resulted in the fact that I've been put into this vulnerable position and why I've ended up in here.

So going back I would allocate, I'd flip it, probably allocate the exact opposite to 12 hours a day to the family and a few hours to my business. I've heard other successful businessmen say that and of course some people naturally do that, don't they? Mothers are particularly good at this aren't they? Because they have to be. They spend time with their children from the minute they're born they come at life from a completely different angle to that which we do.

JR: Tell me, has religion ever played a part in your life?

Lincoln: Yeah, I mean when I said I went to a music school that was actually a chorister school so I sang for myself if you like from the age of seven and then was a musician all my life. I play the piano here in Chapel and particularly when there's a chap here called Richard who plays, who's fantastic far better than me, but when he was on holiday and any days he didn't turn up I would go down and play but yeah I don't necessarily feel the need to go to Chapel. Unfortunately it conflicts with the gym now and so if I do want to spend time thinking about religion or my personal beliefs then I can do that in the comfort of my own apartment for myself.

JR: So I'm trying to imagine a young lad of seven living at home with mum and dad.

Lincoln: Well no, I was sent away to school at seven.

JR: That's my question. Were you sent away?

Lincoln: Yeah, yeah.

JR: How was that then? Hard I suppose but a little bit like this, same types of feelings ?

Lincoln: It may be, somewhere or another somebody was saying you need training and what's going to come one day. I don't know, it depends on what you believe in doesn't it? I'm not so sure about that but I do know it stood me in good stead for the rest of my life after that but that wasn't an easy school.

JR: Had you effectively left home or did you go back home afterwards?

Lincoln: I went back home at thirteen and then left at sixteen and I left there just to go to the biggest city I could find in the vicinity.

JR: And that was your choice?

Lincoln: Yeah, that was my choice. It was my choice, but I didn't get on with my father, he was a pretty brutal character We get on now but at that point the two of us couldn't live under the same roof and so I thought I would go and seek my fortune and left with a hundred quid

JR: I should think he's got as many regrets as you have.

Lincoln: I would hope more. Because he's losing his son isn't he?

JR: Yeah, but did you know how that would impact on his life? Did you have brothers and sisters?

Lincoln: Yeah, yeah, I've got a sister but not particularly close anymore. We were when we were young but she's got you know, drug and alcohol problems She was recovering with those, she's never really worked, she's always been dependent on my parents. I've always been very independent and wanted to do my own thing, my own way. But I was never successful, not till I met my wife and then once I met my wife she gave me the confidence in myself whereas before that I was probably always lacking and looking for parental approval.

JR: I think we all need approval, we all need somebody to say, well done, you're doing okay You're doing alright, keep going, you're doing the right thing.

Lincoln: I find that here with the reading when I'm teaching the guys here just giving them that motivation, patting them on the back and that's what they enjoy and that's why they come back for more and I enjoy it, it's a pleasure.

JR: Do you do any of the other arty things they do in here with the plasticine and the painting and the matches and there's all manner of things you can do in here that I've never done?

Lincoln: You know, I haven't actually and I've bought some matchsticks but then I lent them out, I gave them to somebody because they didn't have any so I'm back to having just glue which isn't much use. But one of the things I have done in here is read prolifically. I've never read in my life and I've read, in the six months I've read 60 books or so.

I'm writing a diary that I want to publish when I'm out I don't think it's enough hours in a day, it sounds ridiculous but I've got my schedule of what I do each week and each day and I make sure that I have that reading time and my time with my kids, time with my wife time with my business colleagues and then I've got my time teaching and then I also work on the servery so I mean it's pretty full on week really Seven days a week Yeah, and then I've got the gym and my exercise every day as well so I suppose that's the important thing isn't it, keeping yourself busy. I'm going to step up to another level and try even harder.

JR: It would be a very easy place to do nothing all day wouldn't it?

Lincoln: Yeah and I think there are people who do that but even when I was in 23 hours a day I'd write a little grid out every single day and write down my exercises that I was going to achieve, types of exercises and then I did a thousand units a day, minimum 5,000 a week some days I'd only do seven, six or seven hundred but you know, press-ups, sit-ups, squats, whatever it was that would add up to a thousand a day and it's fantastic and obviously because you don't drink alcohol here as long as you don't eat too much bread I've probably dropped a stone in weight and I'm feeling the best shape available and I feel the better for it.

JR: I'm happy to hear your comments on reading because you know it's another one of my passions you and I have spent many hours talking about books and so on this prison is very innovative in running the reading course that we've currently been meeting on and so I'm delighted that you enjoyed and perhaps not just at my behest you chose to do it yourself anyway but in some small way we helped you.

Lincoln: 100% but I think with courses you run whilst it was poetry and whilst it was reading it was much more than that because it was a way of meeting fellow inmates that I would never have spoken to inmates that you then end up developing friendships and seeing commonalities and so I would say your courses help with more with mental health than anything and yes I have seen people go from being very, almost not wanting to read ever to reading quite a lot but I think the mental health aspect of your courses is where the real benefit is.

JR: It's a very thin line as you know because you've been there. Every time I come in I bring some tea and some coffee and a few biscuits and it's a very thin line between doing that and some would say well you're just persuading them to come they'll sit there all day and drink your tea and then there's nothing to have a cup of tea and biscuits but we're English aren't we and we let no cup of tea.

Lincoln: But that's not why people come I mean if there were no biscuits or tea or anything like that people would still be there John because it's an occasion I can tell you now and I've told you before that Thursday I would wait all week for that Thursday because that would be the day I was away from those four walls where I was trapped in that cell and you were the first person that would actually ask how you're feeling and what are we going to talk about today and we'd have discussion groups and we would read different newspapers and you'd bring different magazines in and then we would have debates so it is amazing.

JR: Well thank you very much, well don't underestimate it. But you know the story is about you rather than me and I just do my best and I'm sure that anybody coming into prison if they ran the same ethos, if they just tried their best it would stand them in good stead and sometimes when you try your best it goes wrong, mistakes are made we've all got choices and chances in life and sometimes we make the wrong choice and a lot of people in here that will say to me, we just did the wrong thing on the wrong day and it's as simple as that.

Do you know Mr L it's an absolute pleasure talking to you and I think I could probably talk all day but for now I think that's enough so I'm really grateful for you talking to me and thanks for that

Lincoln: Cheers John

Chapter 6

Joshua

Prison is a place where people from all walks of life cross paths, often bringing with them unique perspectives shaped by their backgrounds and cultures. In this conversation, I sit down with Joshua, a young man from the travelling community, whose experiences of prison life, family, and personal growth offer a compelling insight into resilience, adaptation, and the challenges of breaking cycles.

Joshua's story is one of contrasts—between a tight-knit community where family bonds are unshakable and the isolating environment of incarceration. From growing up in a caravan and learning to drive as a child to navigating life behind bars, his journey is shaped by both the strengths of his heritage and the struggles of past choices.

Despite spending a significant portion of his young life in prison, Jordan is reflective about his experiences. He speaks candidly about the stark differences between life on the outside and the regimented existence within prison walls. He acknowledges the pull of familiar patterns but also expresses a strong desire to create a better future—both for himself and, most importantly, for his five-year-old daughter.

This conversation explores the importance of family in the travelling community, the realities of prison routines, and the mental resilience needed to survive and adapt. We discuss education, rehabilitation, and how creative outlets like music and rap give prisoners a voice. Joshua also shares his hopes for the future, recognising the need to distance himself from negative influences and embrace new opportunities.

At its core, this is a story about choices—those already made and those still ahead. It's about the tension between past and future, and the possibility of change even in the most challenging of circumstances.

As we begin, I ask Joshua about his upbringing and how life within the travelling community has shaped him.

The Interview . . .

JR : Hello, how are we doing? We all right?

Joshua: We're fine, yeah.

JR : Now **Joshua**, as I've already said, I don't know you at all. I've no idea how we met. All I really know is you're from the travelling community.

Joshua: Yeah, that's correct.

JR : And I have met very many people from the travelling community in this prison and they've always been kind and gentle with me. So I've never had the slightest problem. But please tell me a little bit about your life. How old are you, for example?

Joshua: Currently I'm, well, 25 I was yesterday.

JR : Okay, happy birthday for yesterday then, yeah?

Joshua: But, yeah, I've been in jail probably about five years in my life so far.

JR : And what do you think about that?

Joshua: It's different, it is really different. It's just, obviously when you're out in the community it's very active, very lively, but it's a completely different kind of setting, you know.

JR : Yeah, of course it is. And I think most people would say that, whether they were travellers or not. Everyone would say this is very different. But one of the reasons we are chatting is simply to show people that, yes, it's different, but it's not impossible to survive. Indeed, many people flourish. They learn a trade or a skill and when they leave here they're different to when they came in, in the rehabilitative culture that we try and help people through with. So take me back a little bit, if you would, Joshua, to your family.

What have you got in the way of family? Mum and Dad, as well as your sisters?

Joshua: Yeah, I've got my mum, dad, my sister and my daughter. She's five years old now.

JR : Right, okay. And does her mum live with you?

Joshua: No, I don't really have much to do with her.

JR : Oh, okay. So you've got the little girl to look after?

Joshua: Yeah.

JR : And your mum does that, I take it?

Joshua: Yeah, my mum does it at the minute, yeah.

JR : Because I think it's true to say that, in many cases, the travelling community from a family perspective is much stronger than those that are not from the travelling community.

Joshua: Yeah, my parents have always said you can count your closest people on one hand.

JR : I think your parents are not wrong.

Yeah. You're not wrong.

JR : I come from a conventional family and I've got a sister that I have nothing whatsoever to do with, because it's too painful to do it. So yeah, I admire you. And also there's some other cultures around the world where they're much stronger on family ties than we are.

So there we are. So mum looks after. Now, in terms of living, do you live in a house or a van? Do you move around?

Joshua: No, I lived on the site in a caravan and I had a chalet. Well, it was a chalet and I was in a caravan next to it. Yeah, yeah. I was probably driving an automatic at the age of seven. **JR** : Were you?

Joshua: Yeah, I was driving a manual at the age of eight.

JR : Now, I've got grandchildren that age and they can't do that. So that's a bonus. And dare I ask about reading? Were you encouraged or can you read?

Joshua: My mum was always a strong reader, so she taught me, but my dad's not so much.

JR : And I wonder what disadvantage that is really, because I've met many people who can't read and write and they don't see it as a disadvantage. They see it as an advantage.

Yeah, they just, well, they get the forms and that written for them.

JR : And you get many people in this prison that can't do it. And in this prison, we've got CD players and we've got books recorded onto CDs. So they needn't be bookless. They can still "read a book" and enjoy that pastime because that's one of the problems, isn't it? Of being in prison. How do you spend your time? What do you do? So talk us through a day, would you? How does it work out?

Joshua: Well, my daily routine, I'd probably get up about six o'clock, just automatic. I'd probably do a little workout and then about half eight they crack the door. And then obviously I'm a domestic on the wing, so I do the cleaning and that. So I run the broom around and mop a little bit, clean the showers out. And then until probably about 12 o'clock when it's mealtime, it's just playing cards or having a nap with the lads and that.

JR : Yeah, yeah. So how much of your day would you spend in your cell?

Joshua: When you first come in, it's quite harsh. I was in Covid as well at that point, it was 23 and a half hour bang up.

JR : So you'd get half an hour out a day to get all your food sorted, to get your exercise and just do your general things on the wing. But if you get a trusted job, you're out a bit more.

Joshua: So at the minute I'm out pretty much as much as I can be.

JR: Good. So it's half eight till 12, bang up till two and then out again at two and bang up again at six. That must play havoc with your mental state?

Joshua: When you first come in, I've been in jail three times now, so it's not new to me, but at first it's a big shock to the system because obviously I was out and about and always going about meeting my mates, doing things, going for meals. But as soon as you're shut in, it's just a different atmosphere. You sort of have to adapt to it to keep the mind keen, stimulate yourself.

JR : Yeah, that's the trouble, isn't it? How do you keep active? And of course there are those people who don't want to stay active isn't there? They just want to sit in their bed and do not a lot.

Joshua: Yeah, and they do not very much at all.

JR : Do you think there's anything you could do in this prison to improve your situation when you leave?

Joshua: I think take on as many opportunities as you can, like the courses, the education. It's free in here, like the gym and that. Exhaust every resource that they put out to you.

JR : Okay, so let's run through them one at a time then. So best way of going forward is the gym, I take it?

Joshua: Yeah, yeah, the gym. Keep your body fit and well.

JR : And how often are you able to go to the gym?

Joshua: This prison's not the best for gym. It's not the worst, though. You can get it twice a week if you're not enhanced, and three times if you are enhanced.

JR : And each time you go, what is it, an hour?

Joshua: Yeah, we get about an hour there, then 10 minutes of a shower and then back.

JR : So you're worn out by the end of it anyway. You probably couldn't do more than an hour, could you? Or could you?

Joshua: Personally, I'd like two hours a time so you can get a bit of cardio out in there, but they just can't be used.

JR : No, and I must admit, being at the other end of the age scale from you, you know, the worst thing in my life would be going to the gym every day. You know, I couldn't live without it because, you know, I've got to safeguard the six-pack, haven't I? And work away. Right, so in an ideal world then, in your ideal world, the gym would be every day?

Joshua: Yeah, every day, every opportunity I could, yeah.

JR : And that helps your mental state as well?

Joshua: Yeah, because when you're working out and trying to make yourself feel better, you feel better yourself.

JR : Yeah, of course. You mentioned education a minute ago. Have you undertaken any education in the prison?

Joshua: Not so much on this sentence, but on my previous ones, I did manage to get my maths, English and, yeah, a couple of things like that in prison. Mentoring and catering.

JR : And did that help you on the outside when you left?

Joshua: The maths and English side of it did, but I kind of just went back into my old ways when I got out the second time. So I didn't really use it. I could have put it to use, but I didn't really do that myself.

JR : I went to university and graduated when I was 49 and I thought, that's handy. I'd always wanted to do it. Have I ever used it? Yeah, I use it every day, but not the piece of paper that says I've done it, just the knowledge that I've gained along the way. So I think when you do something in prison and you learn something, you don't realise how often you use it.

A lot of people come in, obviously they've got bad backgrounds, a lot of people who are in care and that, and then they get thrown in the system. So it is good in that respect, it teaches them basic foundations a lot, doesn't it? Maths particularly. The maths is a big one.

Joshua: And you've never been in care yourself, I take it?

No, I've never been.

JR : And generally I think travellers don't, do they? They look after their own, close-knit families and that.

So in the place where your lodge is positioned, where your home is, are there many of them together in the one place? Is it a nice little community?

Joshua: It depends who's wanted or doing crimes and at the time really. So obviously some people go off and then come back and it's pretty much hit or miss.

JR : The family's there sometimes and then you wake up in the morning and they're gone. I don't want you to paint a picture of travellers being a load of villains moving around the country, because I don't believe they are.

Joshua: No, they're not.

JR : There's a lot of good travellers out there, yeah. I've had guys in here that have said to me, you know, as soon as we're on the out we'll come to your house and we'll repave your front garden and things like that, or take a few trees up or whatever, you know.

And I've employed travellers and they've been wonderful people, so I'm certainly not anti-traveller, but I'm intrigued by the way of life because I've not lived it. You know, my life is so different and over time no doubt my life will come out as well, but yeah, it's amazing.

But I'm intrigued by family, you know, because my family is quite close-knit. Currently I've got a daughter and her two children living in the same house as us and it's built a whole load of new pressures. But these are pressures that exist in the travelling community all the time, aren't they? Because as you said a moment ago, your mum is now looking after your five-year-old.

But she's still there, she's got her own room and that, so. So she's happy?

Joshua: Yeah, she's over the moon.

But she'd be even happier if daddy was with her?

Joshua: Yeah, 100%, yeah. Yeah, I'd be a lot happier if I was with her as well.

JR : So let's talk about that relationship then, shall we? Let's see if we can get some interesting facts out of that, because some would say, well if you have such high regard for your daughter, why would you be involved in a life of crime? Some would say, and I would say, hold on a minute, you know, this is real world here. And people make bad choices.

We all do things that we really regret afterwards.

And I've no interest whatsoever in what got you in here, but one aspect of it must be that you miss your daughter.

Joshua: Yeah, I was missing my daughter a lot. The main aspect is just money, really. You've got to get money to treat them. You want the best life possible for your daughter, so. Yeah. You think it's a shortcut.

JR : And it's not, is it?

Joshua: No, it doesn't work out now.

JR : So I wonder how you learn that lesson, you know, because you quite rightly say there are travellers that find themselves in prison and there are travellers who regress it and they only did it for the money, really.

So yeah, how do you get to that position in life? You know, you must have, who's the role model? Is your dad your role model?

Joshua: I'd say my dad's the man of the house, but my mum gets the final word, so. I always looked up to my granddad, really, and he was very set in his ways, like an old Traveller man is. But yeah, he didn't, he wasn't much for the rules and that, and I guess growing up, I just wanted to be like him when I should have been like he was in the end.

JR : Was your dad ever away and in prison himself?

Joshua: No, my dad's always been around.

JR : And was your granddad?

Joshua: My granddad done a bit of time.

JR : But you find that you look more to your granddad than your own dad?

Yeah, I used to, but obviously the last few years of my granddad's life, he got diagnosed with cancer and that, so he just completely switched around. Of course. He went from being a rogue to a lovable person. I think I need to look towards him really.

JR : Well, I think people can be both. They can be a rogue and they can be a lovable person. I know at least one in my life that falls into that category and never a problem for me, not in the slightest, because they're not going to hurt me.

But you need to have some kind of... You're growing up, you've a little girl now, her role model, you know, is your mother I expect at the moment because you're not there.

Yeah. And you know that your mum will do it right because she did it right for you and your sister, but it's a responsibility that maybe she takes on the chin now, but in 10 years' time maybe she wouldn't be able to.

Joshua: Yeah. Maybe she'll be finding it too much like hard work. So it's my job then to provide stability and... Yeah.

JR : Correct me if I'm wrong, but I think the travelling community generally is a little bit chauvinistic, isn't it? It is the men or the hunter-gatherers, the classic.

Joshua: Yeah, yeah. They go out and earn the money and the wifey stays at home and tends to the house and looks after the children, that kind of thing. Yeah, 100%. A traditional role. Yeah.

JR : But what little I know about the travelling community, I've seen on TV and I've met people in here as well, but funerals and weddings, they're an expensive thing in the travellers world as well?

Joshua: They're expensive and they're massive, yeah.

JR : So are you yet thinking in terms of your daughter's wedding? I mean, I know she's only five, but are you now thinking, well, in 10, 12, 15 years' time I'm going to have a big expense?

Joshua: Yeah, there will be a lot of money going towards that, yeah. But it's not just usually like the daddy would chip in, it'd be the whole family kind of comes together.

JR : Do they?

Joshua: Yeah, they all chip in.

JR : You see, again, it's different to the normal community, isn't it? It's like a pot for all. So when you bring this different way of living, if you like, into prison, what lessons do you need to learn? How do you treat the staff in here and how do other prisoners treat you?

Joshua: Well, there's obviously a hierarchy wherever you go in life, but I think if you show that you can put your guard up and you can look after yourself, then you'd be left alone.

But I've met a lot of nice people in jail as well. Obviously, they're all criminals.

JR : I have too. There's some lovable people in jail, but you just got to basically use your instincts and click out the best for you. So from that respect, you think it's the same as on the outside?

Joshua: Yeah, 100%.

JR : Because I've met people in my working life that I've trusted initially, and they've come back and hurt me. And it's the same in prison. Yeah, 100%. In many ways, you're better off in prison, because if you're on medicine, for example, I've seen the queue every morning for meds.

Joshua: If I want to get meds, if I've got to go to the doctor for something new, it's just impossible. On the other hand, if you want a dentist in here, it's not easy to get one, is it? It's not easy to get one. Obviously, due to COVID and that, there's a big backup. It takes quite a while to get your teeth hooked up. He just tends to put his knee on your chest and rip them out more than you tend to. Yeah.

JR : Well, that's okay, but it doesn't always solve a problem, does it? Leaves you with another problem.

Joshua: Yeah.

JR : So would you sum up your life in here as being bearable? Comfortable?

Joshua: At first, it does seem like it's never going to end and you can't deal with it anymore. But as time goes by, you just got to learn to adapt and you find pleasure in the little things. So the more you get out of it, the more you see and the more you want to do. You just take every opportunity you can, really. I've seen some wonderful examples in here that you never see on the outside. Probably it might be there, but you just don't see it. For example, matchsticks models are crazy, yeah.

JR : I've seen some mad ones. Do you do any of these yourself?

Joshua: I've tried. I'm not really a dab hand at that.

JR : I've seen a lot of great artwork come out of matches.

Okay. So I already know what your art is so ,let's talk about it. Because you're a rap artist, aren't you?

Joshua: Yeah, I like doing that.

JR : How did you get into rap? Because I'm of a generation that thought it was all rubbish until I met you. And then you showed me there was some nice stuff.

Joshua: I think it was just really the social media influence of it. I mean, you've seen people coming from our backgrounds, just flourishing by telling stories about their lives, free lyrics and that. And that's the thing about rap music, isn't it.

JR : And I like telling stories. That's why people call me John the Storyteller. I just like doing it. But I couldn't put it into a song because I haven't got the musical knowledge. Where do you get your musical knowledge from? Do you think it's a naturally gifted thing?

Joshua: I've always been, I always liked music growing up and that. But I ended up meeting one of my friends and he was, he was quite into the rap and that. So I just kind of sat there, listened to him and then took notes and that. And then eventually just, it's like anything, the more you do it, the more you get used to it, the more you do it, the better at it.

JR : But here in prison, how do you absorb your rap music in here? You've got a CD player, I take it?

Joshua: Yeah, I've got a CD player. I'm fortunate enough for money to be sent in and that. Some people don't really get that. But yeah, I ordered a CD player. I've got some instrumental CDs coming, but usually I just put a CD in and ignore the person singing. Yeah, yeah.

JR : And you listen to the music?

Joshua: Yeah.

JR : So the music's more your thing?

Joshua: Yeah, yeah.

JR : Although you write your own rap?

Joshua: Yeah, I write my own lyrics.

JR : So there's a bit of a dichotomy there, isn't there? A bit of two things off at a tangent really. I've listened to some rap music and really enjoyed it, and I'm quite surprised myself that I have. But when you leave here, could you make a career out of rap music?

Joshua: I've tried it in the past. I do hope to be there one day, but it's like everything, it's a long process. You've just got to climb the ladder. I've got a few music videos out, but it's popularity really.

JR : When you see rap artists on YouTube and places like that, they make it look easy, don't they?

Joshua: Yeah.

JR : But how long has it taken them to get there? We never know unless we talk to the people. It is a long struggle. Some people just naturally have a grasp of the audience and that, but some people it does take a long while. Do you think it's a form of music that lends itself more to our coloured friends than it does our side of the water?

Joshua: Yeah, I do think that 100%. I think all people like it, but the main target audience is obviously people in the slums, as you call it, or the backgrounds and that.

JR : And would you say in the Traveller's community that there are more people who enjoy rap than any other music, or is it a general mix?

Joshua: Well, my parents and that, they love the country in my stomach.

JR : Do they?

Joshua: Yeah, a bit of Kenny Rogers, Donny Boy and that.

JR : Oh yeah, well I'm with them then. I'll come to your house and listen then, that's the answer to that. It's different generations, isn't it? It's all different music going through the ages. If you were writing a rap song today, what would you write about?

Joshua: I just like talking about past experiences, life in general, and it depends what kind of setting you're going for.

JR : You mean good experiences or bad ones?

Joshua: It could be both. Obviously, you can start off with some of the bad and then you can turn it into some of the good. It's all about negativity and positivity and showing the journey through that. Yeah, yeah, yeah, and where you're going with the rest of your life.

JR : So there we are. So what stage are you at then? You're on remand at the moment, I know. Yeah, I'm on remand now. But when you get sentenced, at least you know how long you're going to be in prison, out of the frame. That might have some sad connotations, that might reflect it. If you were to get a longer sentence, your brain would immediately go to, well how old's my little girl going to be when I get out?

Joshua: Yeah, that's the first thing you think about. I've been in jail for quite a bit of my daughter's life now, so she's always seeing daddy as a phone, or coming up to see me on my visits. Our main relationship is through the telephone. But yeah, whether you get short sentences or long ones, it's always hard on the family. My dad always says it's those outside riding the stretch just as much as we are in here.

JR : Yeah, of course. And she starts school in September, I take it?

Joshua: Yeah, she does.

JR : Has she already been to school?

Joshua: No, she's done little visits to the big school and that, but she's going up to the big school probably in September, yeah.

JR : So all of my children have gone through this a long time ago. My youngest daughter is 43 now, so we're going back some years, but we've got grandchildren going through it, and I know that those first days of school, those first drawings. When my grandchildren are away on holiday at the moment, and I found a little note that Olivia left me aged eight, and it just said, be careful granddad, love you, see you soon, and a little picture.

And it brought a tear to my eye to be honest, because it's a reflection of the way she feels. Do you get any drawings in from your daughter?

Joshua: I get two cards a week, I send two cards out as well, so we're always writing to each other. Yeah, I get these packs off the chaplaincy, they do little stickers and loads of things just to stick onto the cards and that.

JR : That's great.

Joshua: Yes, as much as we can communicate, there's also, like you said with the matchstick models, there's people who do stuff out of bread and glue, but they mix it together, they make models, and then if you get it signed off you can take it home and give it to them on a visit.

JR : The thing I saw most recently that you might like to try is soap carving.

Joshua: Yeah, I've seen that, yeah.

JR : But I wonder if you did it, whether you would enjoy it, and get better at it.

Joshua: Yeah, I think it's like anything, I think practice makes perfect. Yeah, because in the library there's some models that people have made of soap, and they're just unbelievable. Phenomenal, yeah.

JR : But it's the same with matchsticks. For the reader I might add that the matchsticks don't actually have a head on them, do they?

Joshua: No, it's just the shaft.

JR : So we're not talking about training a load of arsonists up. But the models I've seen are fantastic. I've also seen modelling in bread, where you break the bread down into crumbs and then you reshape it. It's a bit like plasticine in many ways, isn't it?

Joshua: Yeah.

JR : But again, remarkable models. I saw one made of a human brain, and you know on a human brain there's lots of trenches and markings all over it, if you took the skull off first. And you can't imagine sculpting it, but this man did, and it was rather wonderful. So there we are, let's look to the future. Let's look optimistically at where you're going with your life from here.

Let's assume that it goes to trial, and you're found innocent, and the judge says, well thank you Joshua, goodbye. What's going to happen then?

Joshua: Well I keep saying every time I get out, I'm going to make a change, and I keep slipping back into my ways. I think I need to surround myself with people who are going to help me better my life, and to actually try and better my life myself.

JR : Okay, so I'm not wanting to know the crime by any stretch of the imagination, but is it possible if you go back to the same home environment, which obviously you will, is it possible to not have contact with the people that are a bad influence?

Joshua: No, I'd have to move away a little bit.

JR : You would? To get away from it geographically you mean?

Joshua: Yeah

JR : And could you, if you moved away, could you leave your daughter with your mum for a little while?

Joshua: Well at this point, obviously everything's in place, and I've got myself sorted, I'm hoping that she'll come live with me.

JR : Yeah, okay, in the future? And that's the goal really, isn't it?

Joshua: Yeah, that's the main goal.

JR : And that's the thing that will probably keep you out of prison in the future, because you're seeing now that you don't want to be away from her.

Joshua: No, she's growing up too quick and I'm missing her.

JR : So when we talk about rehabilitation in prison, as much as anything, it's what you're going to when you leave. Have you thought about gaining a trade while you're in here, learning to plaster for example, or to tile a wall?

Joshua: I did jump on the plastering course for a little bit, and yeah, it does take my fancy, like I'm not a fan of doing maximum work for minimal return or anything like that.

JR : Not many of us are, but the reality of this world of course is that you've got to start somewhere, haven't you?

Joshua: Yeah, you have, yeah.

JR : Yeah, and so you need to get your head around that first of all, but I think the future, especially at the age you are, you've got your whole life in front of you, you know, you've learnt the lesson, you don't want to be doing this anymore, so there we are.

So yeah, it's an absolute pleasure to talk to you Joshua, so I'm going to tie it up there and say thank you very much my friend, I've enjoyed the conversation, and I hope that anyone reading this has also enjoyed and raised a few points, perhaps changed a few opinions on the travelling community, and I hope that you've enjoyed this chat, so thanks very much Joshua.

Joshua: Thank you very much, I appreciate it.

Chapter 7

Dan

Every person in prison has a story, and often, those stories are far more complex than the crime that led them there. In this conversation, I sit down with Dan, an actor, voice artist, and musician whose life has taken unexpected turns. His journey has seen him move through the disciplined structure of the army, the creative world of theatre, and now, the confines of prison—a stark contrast to the life he once knew.

Dan's story is one of resilience and adaptation. Growing up in a small town in Scotland, he faced early challenges with family relationships, the loss of his beloved grandfather, and struggles with his own identity. Yet, through all of this, he found solace in music and acting; passions that would shape his life and give him a sense of purpose. Even in prison, he continues to find ways to engage with creativity, from writing poetry and books to taking on the role of a Listener, supporting those struggling with the realities of incarceration.

His recent diagnosis of Autism Spectrum Disorder (ASD) has also given him a deeper understanding of himself, explaining behaviours and emotions he had long questioned. Prison has become, in many ways, a reflective period—one where he is piecing together his past, making sense of his struggles, and setting intentions for his future.

As we speak, Dan is open about his experiences—his love for Blackpool as a place of peace, his challenges with loneliness, and his aspirations for life beyond these walls. With a sharp wit and a deep sense of self-awareness, he offers a fascinating insight into life before, during, and after prison.

This is not just a conversation about incarceration; it's about identity, purpose, and the power of the arts to heal and transform. It's about learning from the past and looking toward a future that is still full of possibility.

The Interview . . .

JR: Let's begin by talking about your life, not the prison life but the life that you had before you came in here.

Dan: To start off I have a Scottish accent so I come from a little town in Scotland. My family life was up and down a lot, my real dad disappeared as soon as I was born so I don't really know him but I grew up with a step dad. I was more of a mummy's boy anyway but my hero was my granddad, my "papa" and he's the reason that I got into music and my acting as well. He died when I was 13 and that's when I really started to take my music seriously. I have two younger brothers', both still up and Scotland, I don't hear from them much now due to the relationship between my mum and my first step dad but we're trying to keep in touch as often we can.

As you know I like to go and visit Scotland as much as I can and any excuse will do.

JR: I'll vote for that Dan. Would you say growing up without your real father was ever a problem I mean presumably you can't remember him ?

Dan: I don't remember him I even now I don't know what he looks like even though my mum tried to point him out and a few times but like I say my papa was my hero but he died when I was 13. That's a difficult age for a kid growing up especially you know when you can't talk to mum about certain things, about growing up.

JR: If you don't mind me asking, how old are you now Dan?

Dan: You know I'll be 40 in December.

JR: So we're going back a few years, when your papa died what memories do you have of him?

Dan: Every Saturday we would always go for walks. Just me and my papa that was our time. He actually started to teach me my first drum roll, when he was still capable. So when he took his stroke to give my grandma a break they would come up and stay at mum's for about a week or 2, and tell me stories. I remember my earliest memory and I think this is where my acting started. We went to watch him play, he was doing the Jungle Book, he was the drummer for The Jungle Book and one of the cast member actually came down and tried to drag me up on stage.

But I would not go, "I'm staying right here" but that's where it all started from really. I think my papa's next-door neighbour, because he was in a band as well, he was in a Scottish Curly band. He was a friend; he was also part of the music side of things but his wife was one of the actors on stage and it was her that tried to get me to go up.

JR: I find it difficult to imagine knowing that you've been an actor since why you would refuse it that age. You think it was just your age that was the problem?

Dan: I was pretty young yeah and I think it was I don't have any confidence so I was still pretty much cuddling into my mum, not one to leave her side. She's now cares for a second Step Dad who has dementia.

JR: Okay but the relationship between you and Mum is a bit strange since coming in here.

Dan: I've had a year now to accept that and just deal with it is what it is there's nothing I can do so I try and get on with it.

JR: Really, it's not gonna last forever is it ?

Dan: It's not no. I still wonder about how dad's doing I mean mum you know she's a trooper she won't let anybody else look after him. It's got to be a hard job and as much as I've offered to help, nothing against me, it's not as if she doesn't trust me, she just trusts herself more. Well age is an issue now and I think they both are in their mid to late 50s and Mum slightly older than Dad. But because she was the carer they could move into a disabled house.

JR: So they'll be fine they'll be fine, good job. When you came in here you left behind a pleasant artistic world ?

Dan: I did John. I spent some time in the army when I left school so the prison regime I took to quite easily. Now while I'm here I've got a job as a domestic on the wing and I've actually passed my clearance to start a listener's course which starts tomorrow which I'm looking forward to. But the hardest thing was leaving my family and friends and what makes it difficult is I've got friends in America who I used to keep contact with by email or through social media, but because I can't write to them for all they know I could be dead !

JR: Yes so they're in for a pleasant surprise when you get out. Yeah you've risen from the dead, you might be able to play Jesus Christ perhaps. We should not say that but you never know what the future holds.

Dan: I'd like to grow my YouTube channel because it's the one thing that I'm good at, and because now I've just been diagnosed with autism I've got my mental health to consider. I use YouTube as my way getting away from the problems in the world it gives me a few hours to be somebody else to concentrate maybe on my writing or my music and it gives me that time to just kind of refresh if you like.

JR: Yes and help you through this journey. So you told me something before we started this conversation about a recent diagnosis you've had and what was that again ?

Dan: it's ESD autistic spectrum disorder.

JR: How do you think that affects ?

Dan: It makes more sense of how I am the way I am because sometimes if you'll be talking to me and all of a sudden I'll just switch off for no reason it's nothing against you or what you are saying, but I'll just completely shut off and just blank everything, I'm going to own little world according to the psychologist I score quite high on the "paranoia obsessive avoidance scales" which is the problem and it could be treated. I'm not a psychologist but I think it said on the form something along the line of some sort of Aspergers.

JR: I know from previous meetings you've written some wonderful poetry.

Dan: Thank you.

JR: One that always comes to my mind is the Blackpool and I know that Blackpool is a special place for you isn't it ?

Dan: It's my go-to happy place.

JR: Why is that ?

Dan: Do you know when we had covid I went almost every month with my mates. When I'm there I'm not thinking about what's happened in the past and I'm not worried about is in the future I'm literally there for the entire day living in the moment and it does literally refresh my batteries and because it's next to the ocean as well it's just so calming. We'd leave Shrewsbury about half past 7 get to the park about half past nine and we'd be there till 9 o'clock at night because with the park sometimes closing at six we would go for dinner and just sit on the front just watching the sun go down. It gives me a sense of peace as well.

JR: I know Blackpool a little bit and I resonate with what you're saying I think the seaside via Blackpool or anywhere else is a calming influence so if you're inclined to be a little bit concerned or worried it's always helpful in the same way that walking through a forest has the same affect.

Dan: It's that getting back to nature in a way isn't it and it is yeah because Mum and Dad lived by the ocean as well I just fell in love with it because the hours can just fly by even though you're sat there for about 3 hours it just doesn't feel like that long.

JR: Have you got a favourite ride ?

Dan: Yes, the Pepsi Max Big 1 which is ironic because I don't like heights and the first drop is 235 ft high, it's scary but even then I've got to sit on the left hand side of the car because that's where the stairs are whereas if I'm sitting on the other side it's just a complete drop ! And I'm into the movement and that's something that must come from your autistic spectrum situation. But I do tend to have OCD as well that's usually like a security thing you know I've got to maybe push the door three times to make sure that it's locked even though I know it's prison.

JR: I must admit I'll have a bit OCD in prison as well because I obviously hold keys and wander around and I have to make sure the doors are locked. So how do you spend your days in here then, you tell me, you're a cleaner on the wing but it's not 24/7 job is it ?

Dan: No, well I've started writing another book and well if there's a good film about 9 o'clock I'll sit and watch that but usually I tend to find that what I'm locked up I've had my lunch I'll tend to work on my book a bit and now I've got this course to focus on as well.

JR: Okay so let's talk about the book then when you say another book have you had one published ?

Dan: I've not had one published and I'm still working on my autobiography. The only problem is because I'm not doing it on a computer, I keep remembering things somehow and then go back and fit this bit in here and then rewrite the rest. It's just a case of trying to remember where everything goes, so that's still and work in progress but the first one is finished.

I've actually written a short story which is finished okay it's only about three pages long ! Then there is the book of poems that I did with yourself I'm looking to get that published as well, we can do that when my short story is finished.

JR: That will give you a sense of achievement because I think sometimes we go through life, and I'm as guilty as anybody, that you take stock and you think what have I achieved so far what have I done in my life, and I'm much older than you and I'm certainly thinking "what I'm doing, how am I going to be remembered" ?

Dan: I'm not one that goes looking for praise for me I feel I've not achieved much I don't anything.

JR: But you've got your YouTube channel, you've got your book, you do your music and you've been doing your for 26 years you've been in musical theatre for 10 years that's more than enough achievements.

Clearly you have made a bad choice somewhere along the line and finished up in here but that's not going to last forever there's going to be a life outside that you can go back to, no reason, none at all. I take your point about your friends in America though because these are friends that you talk to you through social media and emails and all the rest it's not possible in here is it ?

Dan: It's not no and it does play on my mind that they think that I'm possibly dead because they do not know about all that stuff about my mental health and they do know that it was quite bad.

JR: They are in for a pleasant surprise then. When I get people say you should only worry about something you can do something about so you can't do anything about that at the moment. Anyway it will test the friendship won't it ? You've been in here over a year now, crossed that year mark, so you said it's your sentence review around Monday.

Dan: Whether that goes ahead or not, we shall have to see, because the courts have kept pushing that date back for the past 3 months so if they push this one back again that doesn't help my mental health because it's like I just want to finish with this okay.

JR: So the day you get some bad news when you're in here you're in your pad you're sharing with somebody, how do you cope with it ?

Dan: Myself I tend to go quiet even though the pad mate does know something's wrong he won't talk about. Last night he asked me " do you want a cup of tea yeah"

I was silent okay and in fairness all credit to him he will just leave me to my own devices for about an hour and so then he asks me again. As time goes on I'll start to open up a bit so the friendship is a supportive one. It gives me a sense of responsibility as well because obviously I've been his pad mate now for about a week he's a stroke victim so obviously you need to help. That gives me that extra responsibility and I feel like I'm doing something for somebody else as well.

JR: This is your listener function, so tell me a little bit about this business because people on the outside will think well surely everybody listens don't they ? But no, there is a role for a person in prison and it's called a listener what does a listener do?

Dan: They're basically do the same job as the Samaritans do. They're trained by the Samaritans and what they're doing is they are basically here to provide help for somebody who's really struggling inside. Maybe someone is here for the first time, they don't know the regime, they're missing a family, or they may feel in a really bad place like I was at first. It's our job to give them that extra bit of comfort, take them to a safe space, perhaps a cup of tea or coffee and just basically let them pour the heart out. So with some of that by saying if you need to be a friend yeah that would be a good place you get to know these people.

JR: But how are you going to cope if you are friends with somebody that needs a listener and the friendship goes on for some weeks or months and then he starts self-harming or even worse how you gonna cope with the upset that they might cause to you ?

Dan: Well I haven't been in that situation myself, I don't know how to deal with it, you know I know what words to use to come with understanding, I don't completely understand but I sympathise because there are a lot of people who think people self-harm for attention and it's not always the case. You don't know what's going on somebody's head. I've got some on the wing who admit to self-harm and I don't have any judgement so if you want to talk, yes he knows me as a humorous guy I will say maybe give them a second chance and say don't do that again. But he knows that if you really need somebody to talk though I am there, because I've been through it and I find it always helps if someone's experience themselves they're the best people to talk.

JR: I think you're right because I've done a mental health awareness course and I can see some trigger points, although I've never suffered it myself and as you know a lot of what I do in prison is associated with loneliness and loneliness is a huge problem in prison. Have you suffered that or have you seen any others who suffer with loneliness ?

Dan:. I have John, I have suffered myself and the toughest part of suffering from loneliness is when you're in a group of people. Because I've done that and felt that from the outside as well and you do tend to see others, that's because they tend to be a bit more withdrawn and quieter even in a group it's like they're watching people talking but they're not.

JR: I can see they're not joining in, in my poetry groups. I've seen you in the room but you're in the corner writing and it's your way of coping isn't it ?

Dan: And it seems to work, it does because even when you're with a group of friends and someone cracks a joke it can be overwhelming and you just need that time to just step back and for me it was right in my poetry.

JR: Let's think about your school days. You left school and your life changed?

Dan: I genuinely didn't have a clue so when I left school the opportunity for me to try out the army came across, I actually wanted to join the RAF but my step dad said "try the army" because the training is much easier. So I signed up to be a driver for the Scottish Regiment and my training started. They couldn't have sent me further away from home but it was my first time away from home I got really home sick so I did my basic training and came back home again.

JR: We spoke earlier about loneliness, would you say that was a very lonely time of your life ?

Dan: It was because I got bullied a lot at home by my step dad, he was quite violent especially if he had a drink. I had ben bullied a lot at school right so I didn't have many friends that's why I got involved with a lot of school activities I became a prefect. I would show the new first year's around when they came up to High School I did that for 2 years. I tried to help out you know when there was a show on for the sound and light and so I tried to get involved as much as activities occurred because I felt as though I preferred my own company. I think this was because I did have trust issues.

JR: Was this leading you into your acting career ?

Dan: My acting career actually came by accident. I was 31 and I had done music since I was 13 so that was always an ongoing thing so effectively it was my passion. When I was 31 I was diagnosed with mental health problems. There was a lot of things going on at home and including having lost two children through miscarriage. One of my friends was actually doing rehearsals for a show called an evening of Rogers & Hammerstein and the show was to raise money for a local church.

And she said to me that we're looking for a drummer why don't you come along to with her so it's on a Monday night and help us out ? Okay, fair enough, so I had a little drum kit I could take a long, did my rehearsals and the Director said I want to hear you singing ! Believe me I tried every trick in the book to get out of that I will not lie, I don't like my voice, I sound like a goose. When I say "no" he said "no not having any of it" so he gave me "My Favourite Things" from Sound of Music.

So I just rattled the song as soon as you like and he was like a kid at Christmas he said "right you're doing that in the show. How I just love that you've got the Scottish accent you're singing and we're going to give you another song to do as well". And that was how my singing career started because there was songs on there that didn't require me to play drums so if I wasn't singing and I wasn't drumming I was maybe acting a little bit on stage. A year later he trained me up to be a Director and I had more of a role in The Show as well and it just grew and grew.

Now I've got my own YouTube channel where I've got my own show that I did with my two friends. I'm looking to continue that and as I think I found my calling to be fair

JR: You think he came into your life by pure chance ? He must have seen something in you that you didn't see in yourself

Dan: More like he heard something, I didn't mean that, I didn't even see myself because it literally started with singing. I don't, I can't, I don't, like singing. I hate the votes on The Voice.

JR: But he obviously heard something, and he was good for you.

Dan: It was yeah because I spent a lot of time in my own little world at home anyway so I think having done that I gave me the natural acting ability I needed to tease out the parts on stage even though they weren't speaking for us you know.

JR: And you obviously had a relationship with a lady for her to have two miscarriages. I've never suffered that in my life but I have a daughter that has so I know it's a very traumatic experience; do you think that was meant to be ?

Dan: I think so now yes because I still hated who I was as a person back then and now, accepting that I'm bisexual and sharing that with a friend who's been in the same boat, who's in here, as well he's helped me to open up about it because I have known it since I was 13. I feel as though if my papa had was alive a little bit longer I could have spoken to him about it because even though I was a mummy's boy it's just something that you don't feel comfortable talking to your mum about.

JR: I wouldn't have felt comfortable talking to my mother either. But I think generations are changing all that aren't they ?

Dan: They are yeah, it's the schools that are helping along the way.

JR: So, you weren't aware of that situation when you left school ?

Dan: No, because I was born in the early 80s so back then it was still a bit of a taboo subject so yeah you had to keep it quiet and because obviously now since it's an open subject it's like there's not so much of an issue now.

JR: And so it should be.

Dan: I stole because I spent so many years hiding it that was all I knew and it started to eat away at me and I got into this relationship with another girl, hoping that, believe it or not, I thought it would change me. I thought it would be such an issue then but it wasn't the case we were going to have two kids she miscarried both of them, which was a better pill to take because no parent should outlive the child yeah but looking at it now it's like maybe it was meant to be. It would be a difficult topic for my little fantasy "why is Daddy not with us anymore" ? That would have been a tough one.

JR: But for your own mental health as well. Maybe you were living a lie.

Dan: I was actually to be fair.

JR: And you will not be the first, and you certainly won't be the last. There are very many people that live a different life to the one they really intended to live and sexuality quite rightly nowadays is talked about openly in schools and that's the right way we're going forward I think.

Dan: It is and it was one of the documentaries I was planning to cover on my YouTube channel because before I came in here. I was working on a script to talk about mental health to make it more of an open subject because there's a lot of people in the world of different opinions about mental health. I split people into three groups, the first group of people who are just completely ignorant about it they don't want to know it's not something they wanted to discuss. The people in the second group aren't necessarily ignorant about it but they're frightened to ask just in case it causes upset, and then you've got a few people that are in the third group who completely understand where you're coming from.

JR: They've learned about it, they understand and they want to try and help where they can. I had a the poetry group in another prison a couple years ago with the transgender girl. It was a men's prison and at the end of the course she said to me "you're alright you are John you get it don't you" and I think I do although many of my generation, and as you know I'm 75 now so I'm no child, would not understand. The vast majority would not have any conversations about it, would want to brush it under the carpet if it happened in their family would not defend anybody in that position. They would say no, if you're born this way or this and if you brought up as that way you're that. But I think it's Society nowadays we need to accept there are any number of different people on that spectrum and yeah I don't think any of them deserve any less respect than any other.

Dan: No they don't and I think hopefully people can't start to be more open about it because I mean I get it there's always going to be that fear of judgment yeah that's always going to be there but I think society now is just, it's more open than what it was you know, and there are professionals out there that can help get that ball rolling.

JR: I think you're openness and your ability to talk about it Dan is wonderful.

Let's talk about the future let's talk about where your life's going whether you get sent home next week or whether it's another couple of years whatever it might be there will come a point when you're released what do you think you'll take from this prison when you leave what happy memories ?

Dan: I think the friends that I've got in here have been quite long lasting you know, as well I think the overall experience is what I'm going to take away because to me this is like the bottom of the ladder you've lost everything you're having to start again. It's like, that I know what that's like I know not to make the same mistakes again and sometimes you know I needed to come here to learn that. Probation can help you know as well but I think being here it's like well I know what this life is like I know where it's like having lost the family so I know to learn from it.

But memories, happy memories as well. Like your poetry classes I never saw myself as a poet but now I've got about 25 poems and a folder just waiting to be published when I get out but my goodness did we enjoy it.

JR: Yeah we had a good laugh not least because you got it. The best bit as well, that's fine whatever you like to call poetry, you know at the end of the day it's about mental health and giving people some pleasure in life.

There are many people in the acting fraternity that have served time and then gone on to be very successful actors so I don't think this is the end of the world and if you learn from it then it's a great place to be.

Now there are those reading to this who don't like to think of people in prison having any kind of pleasure because they think no, they've done the crime they need to serve the time.

I'm not one of them, that's not what I do. I try to keep people looking positively to the future. So I can see people leaving prison a better person for the experience. Not that I would recommend everybody to come in here for the experience, but if you find yourself in prison I hope you learn about yourself so that you know the pitfalls you know what to avoid you know how to cope with it.

Chapter 8

Joe

Success is rarely a straight road. For some, it's a winding path filled with detours, setbacks, and moments of reckoning. Joe's story is one of those journeys—one that begins with an unconventional childhood, moves through a turbulent youth marked by crime and incarceration, and ultimately arrives at a place of redemption, purpose, and community impact.

Today, Joe is the founder of a thriving social enterprise that repurposes and recycles IT equipment, providing opportunities to young people and disadvantaged communities. But his story doesn't start in boardrooms or business pitches—it starts in the arcades and streets of Scarborough, where he learned early how to hustle and survive. With a father who was a natural entrepreneur and a mother who provided grounding and wisdom, Joe grew up with a blend of business instinct and curiosity. But a restless energy—later diagnosed as ADHD—led him down the wrong path, resulting in a cycle of crime, prison, and self-destruction.

The turning point came not in a prison cell but in a moment of self-realisation, staring out over the same cityscape he had known a decade earlier, with nothing to show for the years that had passed. That was the moment he decided to stop making bad choices in good circumstances. From that decision came a transformation—not just in his actions but in his purpose.

Now, Joe channels his energy into creating opportunities for others, ensuring that young people facing disadvantage don't fall into the same traps he did. His journey is one of resilience, reinvention, and the power of finding the right path—one where success isn't just about personal gain but about giving back to those who need it most.

This is the story of a man who turned his past into a tool for change, proving that no matter where you start, it's where you choose to go that defines you.

The Interview . . .

Stories From the Inside Out

JR: Now, this afternoon, it's my pleasure to talk to you, Joe. I know you've got a business up in the north of England. I know it's very successful.

And I know that you're giving some opportunities to a lot of young people that they otherwise might not have. You're helping people with their life experiences and you're taking them down a route, which I'm guessing is very different to the route you had at their age. So I'm interested in knowing where it all began.

But I'm also interested in telling people, from the rooftops, if you like, we are talking to an extremely successful businessman who has done some real work in the community. And it's for the benefit of others that he dedicates his life nowadays. So welcome, Joe.

Joe: Good afternoon. Thank you so much. I'm so happy to hear somebody say that about me. And I'm proud to be that person now, so thank you.

JR: So take me back to where it all began, Joe.
I've no idea how old you are by the way, I would guess you're in your 20s, are you?

Joe: I'm 54 now. I was born in 1970 around the birth of our first home computers and video cassette recorders, top loaders and tape decks and all the rest of that. And I suppose where I came as a kid, I had a fascination with taking things apart. So I took apart a ZX Spectrum 48K because it used to make lots of noise and you couldn't silence it and I wanted to play on it after bedtime.

My parents were quite strict and quiet, you know and so I figured out how to open it up and I was amazed by this electronics inside it. I figured out where the noise was coming from, cut the wire like a bomb disposal expert and that was it. It was a fascination from that moment. It was a fascination with all things inside machines. But my mum and dad, they were hard workers, I was a latchkey kid.

So they'd come home from work in the pub or wherever and I'd be completely immersed in a project, for example taking the videocassette apart. I'd be sat in the front room on the floor, cross-legged and they'd just walk through the door and it'd be quite military really. I knew everything, where it was all going. But yeah, they'd walk home and bust me.

And my dad was quite strict, there was always a consequence. There was a lot of consequence to my actions as I was growing up.

JR: You were growing up in a house with a mum and dad, any siblings brothers or sisters?

Joe: No, no, my dad was a taxi driver, a del boy, a marketer. When you say marketeers now, not marketing.

He used to go to events and markets and shows. My dad was the guy that you'd see one person selling and shouting stuff and they'd have a crowd around them and they'd be doing some shampoo, some liquid that removed the oil from the carpet, some miracle stage remover or magnetic window cleaners on either side of them. Well, that was my dad.

JR: Would we call him an entrepreneur nowadays?

Joe: He was very much an entrepreneur. Very, very much. People used to come to the house to flog him stuff and they'd always leave with something that he flogged them.

He'd go to the shops, he'd go to Dixon's and Curry's and say, OK, I want a microwave, I want a fridge and I want a TV. How much are you going to give them off me? Because if you don't, I'm going to go down to the next door and ask the same question. He used to call him Mr. 10% and that was my dad.

And I used to be his sidekick, his underling. Because I used to get into a lot of trouble, so I'd either be sat in the passenger seat in the taxi or I'd be accompanying him to one of these events and one of these stores and one of these places. And he used to stick umbrella hats on my head and get me to do little side hustles and stuff.

But more importantly than anything, I didn't realise it at the time, he used to, when we set up events and stages in the stores, he used to go around all of the staff, all of the cleaners, all of the cooks, all of the security guards and introduce himself and give them all a business card and make friends and break bread with them. And I always used to wonder why he did that. And then later on in life, he told me, now, if you always work with the working-class staff in any organisation, in any place, these are the people that you need and they will come to your aid when you have a problem or you have a crisis or something's going on.

Not your senior management seat, no, your boots on the ground. And he taught me to actually work with the people around us and value those people around us. But I used to get into a lot of trouble.

I've been recently diagnosed as ADHD. And it makes sense. Back in the day, I was just called a fidgety mischievous.

I wouldn't listen, I wouldn't understand. I was answering everybody's comments before they'd even finished saying them. You know, I had that look in my eye where it's like, come on, come on, I know what you're going to say.

My mum and dad couldn't handle that. And the school couldn't handle that either. It was pre-mental health and wellbeing. So I ended up getting bullied at school and getting picked on. I had psoriasis, I was quite covered in it. I was quite easily picked on at school.

So I grew up in Scarborough, North Yorkshire. So I was next to an arcade on the seafront. I found this fascination with electronics and with computer games and video games.

And I was getting picked on and bullied and I didn't like school because I didn't fit into it. So from around 12 or 13, I spent all of my time in the arcades. I spent all of my days down on the seafront. And I became a hustler. I worked out how to make a living out of the tourist industry, how to make a living inside the arcades. And anybody that's done it, they'll all recognise it.

How you can make a living yourself if you're clever and quick-minded and amongst all the tourists as they're going around, spending all of their disposable income. Yeah, you help them. You signpost them and you get a cut of their profits and you get a cut of their winnings when you help them win.

JR: Yes. Okay. Right, mum. What was mum? You said you were a latchkey kid.

Joe: My mum, yeah. My mum, she made soft toys as a living. She worked for Scarborough Soft Toy Manufacturers and she grew up being a seamstress.

But my dad was very routine and very military. He was a survivor from the War. He was in that. He was quite stern and quite physical with us and quite not, well we didn't really have conversations. We didn't really have a relationship. It was just very much you and me.

This is what I'm doing. But we all lived separate lives. But my mum, my mum was very grounded. My mum was very... She was a hippie in the 60s and 50s. I have a photo of her.

She's got... She's pregnant with me. And she's got flowers painted onto her face. And yeah, she's on some substances or something or other anyway. But she used to take me for long walks and long talks. And she'd explain to me some of the things that my dad did and why he did it and what the circumstance was. And she's rationalised.

And I've had questions in life like, why is school being like this? Why are people being like this? Why is... You know? And she'd actually talk to me about... And we'd go on miles and miles of walks together. And she would rationalise some of the things in life. So I had an entrepreneurial set and a driven set and a kind of mentality of, if you don't go out and do it, then you're not going to get it.

And a drive about it from my dad. But quite strict from behind it, quite monetary. He taught me the value of money. He taught me the value of work. He taught me the value of messing up, you know, and what the consequences of it was. And then I had my mum on the other side sort of teaching the ethics and the morals and the kind of joining the dots into it.

But it still wasn't enough for me. I still... I was one of those kids, the rebels, the rebellious kids. You know, fuck they, fuck you. It's like, no, I know better. I'm brilliant. No, you're all wrong. I'm right, you know? And I ended up getting into crime. Let me start. OK.

JR: You're showing to me absolutely ADHD. This is not an interview. This is Joe telling me his life story. And as you tell it, you're asking questions and I can't ask you questions because you're going so fast. So to summarise your childhood, let's say up to the age of 16, it was a happy childhood.

Joe: Pretty happy, yeah.

Joe: But what I was trying to touch on was I kept getting in trouble. From like age 13 on 14, I started nicking at school. I started nicking in town. I'd get the police coming home every other day. My mum and dad would try and put punishment in place, but it never worked. I'd either run off out the window or, you know, I'd put up with it but then crack on as soon as I got back home.

JR: What kind of crime did you get involved in as a teenager?

Joe: Petty theft, nicking car stereos. You could get into cars with the back of a teaspoon. You could literally get into the locks of them back then, especially minis.

So yeah, robbing car stereos, nicking money from people. Yeah, petty theft.

JR: Did you put the money to good use? What did you use this money for?

Joe: Down the arcades.

JR: So you didn't build up a portfolio of a rich bank balance or anything like that?

Joe: No, no. It was all, it was in one hand, out the other straight away.

JR: There came a point, I suppose, where the police got fed up and they nicked you properly.

Joe: When I was 15, so I'd been working for a milk run. I was a milk lad. And the day before payday, the day before when everybody puts the money out, I'd gone round while that morning, sorry, the payday was on. I'd got up an hour or two earlier and gone round and stolen all the money and then went on the milk run. And I couldn't work out how they sussed it was me. Of course it was me. Of course it was, I'm the only person who knew where they were. Wasn't it a difficult case to crack for the police?

And then I ended up going around and nicking milk from doorsteps and trying to sell it to news agents and all the rest of it. And I actually got caught with about 24 bottles or so walking down the street in carrier bags. And the police just pulled me up, yeah. They said, where are you going with all that milk? It was like seven o'clock in the morning.

JR: The driving force to all this was a need for you to earn money, get money one way or another.

Joe: Yes, one way or another to get money.

JR: You weren't intent on buying loads of drugs or alcohol or anything like that. You were intent on playing the one-armed bandits.

Joe: Video games more. I was playing video games a lot.

JR: So at what point did they lock you up?

Joe: They gave me a warning and a suspension and I got into so much trouble with my mum and dad. And then they decided from my 16th birthday that in the next street, through a friend of the family who had an accommodation there, that they were going to get me a flat. And on my 16th birthday, I moved out.

JR: Did you feel rejected?

Joe: No not rejected, it was just that they couldn't handle me. I was bringing too much shit on the door. I was bringing too much trouble back to the house.

JR: And did you understand that? Huh? Did you understand what you were doing?

Joe: Yeah, yeah. I understood it, yeah. Yeah. I couldn't stop it. It was part of my DNA, yes.

JR: Which is working to your advantage nowadays. But in those days, not so much.

Joe: Oh, in those days, it was so easy. I signed on, I got a YTS, a youth training scheme. Yeah, yeah. And then we got our pay checks sent by the housing. And then I actually had to go and cash the pay checks myself, the rent checks. And yeah, of course, I went down to the arcades with it. Yeah, yeah.

I built up a problem there with it. And then my mom used to come around every other day and sort of clean up, tidy up. And it was a combination of them still trying to support me, but being in my space. And then having debts mounting because I was cashing the rent checks in and not paying the rent. So I ended up just doing a runner to the next town. One day, I just disappeared. I went from Scarborough to Bridlington. Yeah, and I just ran away.

And this was back in the time when you could walk into a job straight away, literally. And that same day, you could turn up in the morning and be working for them in the afternoon. And same with accommodation. You could sign up and get a property and be housed that day and then take your on good faith. Everybody took everybody on good faith. It was awesome.

But I spent the next five or six years there, ripping people off, ripping landlords off, promising the earth and not delivering anything. And then the crimes got worse, and I actually ended up in court. I ended up in cells. So my first one was a YOI Youth Offender Institute, Hatfields. Yeah, I was in Hatfields.

JR: Where is it?

Joe: Doncaster, I think.

JR: It's not too far from home, then?

Joe: Yeah, not too far.

JR: Did mum and dad come and visit?

Joe: Yes, yeah. My mum and dad visited. They came and brought me a parcel, yeah, and supported me as much as they could. But she said, we're disappointed in you, but we've always loved you.

JR: You weren't a fan, but you were always loved. There's a lot of people that I talk to that can't say that. You know, they've come from a miserable background. Their parents have knocked them about. They've abused them.

Joe: Oh, my dad knocked us about. Yeah, he abused us.

Yeah. That was what they were blaming on their criminal... No, it wasn't their fault. I became on towards. But I was already on that track as soon as I came out the gate, yeah. They used to call me Wellington as I was a baby because I had these wellies on and I figured out in a pushchair how to wheel it backwards with my wellies. And I'd scoot off around the arcades.

My mum met my dad in the arcades. He was a mechanic, an arcade mechanic. And she moved to Scarborough and I was three months old. So at three months old, I'm whizzing myself around this arcade. The truck chased me fine. I think that was an indication of my mantra.

JR: Okay, so then your prison career began.

Joe: Yes, yeah. And I started doing commercial dwellings, commercial and dwelling burglaries. Yeah, I figured out how easy it was to get into places and get stuff and get off, you know. Fucking bad, that was terrible. Sometimes they caught you. Yeah, and I'd get caught all the time.

JR: So you were revolving doors, at the prison? So you did what you knew you'd done before and you did it again.

Joe: And I went back again, yeah, seven times. Yeah, seven custodial convictions. Nineteen convictions, yeah.

JR: What was the turning point then, Joe? What was it that happened in prison?

Joe: So I've got this as well, yeah. In 2000, I've been moving around all over the country. I've been to Manchester, Leeds, Liverpool, all over. Mostly in the north. I went to London once, didn't like it too fast. But previously, about 10 years before, I was in Hull in the Salvation Army.

Their Salvation Army, there's a tower block and it looks over the docks. And 10 years later, I was back in the same tower block on the same floor, not in the same room, but looking out over the same view. And I had nothing to show, nothing in my pockets, nothing in my possessions.

But I'm back in the same place looking over the same view. And it was just almost like an epiphany of how did I get myself back here? And how has this come about? And I realised it was by a series of bad choices, series of making wrong choices in the right places. And I made a commitment to myself then to stop.

I know it sounds really simplistic this, but to stop being a dickhead, to stop making the wrong choices, to stop actually when I'm given a circumstance and I'm left on my own in a room, is to not go through people's pockets or start going through drawers or whatever. Stop making bad choices in good circumstance.

JR: Absolutely the right thing to do, Joe. We talk about choices and chances. You know, I've written a book to that effect. But that's what it comes down to, you know.

How long do you want to continue? That word want, how long do you want to continue in the lifestyle you've got? Or what is your desire for change? Do you realise that this can't go on? And so many people at different stages of their life come to the same conclusion that this is pointless at the end of the day. You know, I'm getting too old for this crap or whatever. Anybody that's been remanded, anybody that's either waiting for sentence or waiting for a court hearing, has been on remand.

Joe: I've been on 23 and a half hour lock up. You all think, every single time we sat in the cell, what the hell am I doing here? Why am I back here again? I'm not going to do this again. I'm not going to get out. And we do, that's when the revolving door comes in. Is that great?

JR: How did you get on in prison, Joe? Was it a worry to you or what was it a like?

Joe: It was alright. I was picked on and bullied to some extent in the same way because again, psoriasis, they used to nickname me flaky. Yeah, that was my nickname. But I used to, I joined in, I'd learned that, it's like water off a duck's back by then. I've been homeless. I've sold Big Issue. My humility and humanity have both come equal to each other. I used to say to the lads, well, you're looking at 10 years. I'm looking at getting out in a month. How are you doing that? Because I've been posting myself out bit by bit.

You know, you join in with the banter and you'd actually make joke with it and become one with it. So I didn't like the isolation. I didn't like being locked up, banged up all that time.

It's the worst feeling in the world when a door closes and you can't open it. Horrible. But I was stuck in a cycle.

I didn't know any other way of doing it until I'd reached that epiphany, until I'd reached that point of realisation where I think internally I was ready and that I didn't want to go back and my subconscious was saying, no, no, you're going to, it's just going to scale up. It's going to start growing. It's going to get worse.

You're going to get involved in some crime that's going to put you in for eight to 10 years and you're going to come out a changed person, a completely changed person.

JR: Do you think the prison helped you when you came out for the final time? You're there at the door. They've just released you. You're a free man again. Has the prison helped you at that point to know where you're going with your life?

Joe: No, they didn't. There weren't systems in place. There were some prison officers that cared and wanted to do well, but they were trapped within a system that just produced numbers and management. They were just managing people. And there were some who didn't care. And there were some that did care. They're jokingly say, see you in six months, you know. We'll see you in a few weeks. You'll be back.

JR: So I'm Joe now. I'm you. I'm standing at the gates there. I've got the world before me. I'm determined not to come back. What did you do with your life at that point? Where did you go to ? How did you start moving?

Joe: I moved away from everything. I moved away from everything that I knew and I had to reinvent myself and start again. I moved to Manchester. I came to Manchester. And I thought city, a city. I've got to find my place in a city.

In towns and small places, I'm too fast for this. It's too slow for me kind of thing. What would I be like in a city? I absolutely thrived. I was right.

JR: Joe, the skills you've got now, how do you acquire them? Is it simply through curiosity or did you go and get a qualification or how does it work?

Joe: The beginning was curiosity and self-taught, but now I went off and got qualifications. I went to City College Manchester and became an IT practitioner at level three. Yeah. So I've done my training. I've done my certification and then I've self-taught, learned and administered stuff and done more training since. Okay. We never stopped learning. We never stopped training.

JR: No, no, of course not. But there comes a point, you're now running a very successful social enterprise. So when you're making a decision about your business, you now run, I know, a very successful social enterprise. What made you choose to be a social enterprise as opposed to a sole trader where you could keep all the profits for yourself?

Joe: Balance. You have to balance out the beginning, my first half of my life. I was a liar. I was a cheat. I was a thief. I wasn't a nice person. You couldn't trust me.

JR: And you wanted to garner that trust and respect from the people around you ?

Joe: And now that I've got a position and purpose, I could have took bank loans and got hired staff and gone down different routes for this. I know that. But I thought, no, I use this quote quite often, like Kevin Costner's field of dreams.

I thought, no, if I build it with the community, they will come and they will use it and they will be a part of it. I've learned about co-creation and co-production and person-cantered values. So I wanted to embed the community in this to make that happen.

I understood the area that I'm in as well is second to worst deprivation, areas of deprivation in the country. So the community will rise to this challenge out of need, out of want, out of actual, out of their own heart strings. They want to come and do this because it's them that's it affecting.

So I figured, no, if I build it with the people around us, rather than that route, it'll make for a better result at the end of that theory of change.

JR: No, I'm sure you're doing the right thing, Joe and doing it very well, so yeah, I'm sure. But I can see now how it all fits into a picture here. So where are we today then? I know you've just recently moved to new premises. So tell me a little bit about the place.

It's a town centre, isn't it?

Joe: So yeah, we're inside the shopping centre. We're inside a nearly 4,000 square foot unit within the marketplace shopping centre. And we've just celebrated our three years anniversary and opened the centre with the leader of the Labour Council with us.

And more importantly, we've reached 30 tonnes collected and diverted from landfill. We've put back into the community around 2,000 devices. We spent over three and a half thousand hours with volunteers and placements. And we currently have 22 T-level students placed with us learning about recycling and refurbishment for the next generation. We deliver courses, we go to schools, we do prison workshops. It's the ITAD industry.

So ITAD is Information Technology Asset Disposal or Distribution, which we're an ITAD model, but with social values. So we class ourselves as social recyclers where we don't maximise the profits, we don't make a load of money off the laptops and the units that we provide to the community. They start at £50 and they don't go over £200.

We make it so that it's reachable. But we want the community to be a part of that process to make it reachable, if that makes sense.

JR: Yeah, of course it makes sense. I think it's a very good thing to be thinking about. Do you mind me touching a bit on your personal life though, Joe? Are you married with family yourself now?

Joe: I'm married with five children. Yeah, that was another anchoring, defining point in my life, is I needed to go off and find a ready-made family somewhere I could slot in and be a part of something. But I had no idea where to go to until I found online dating. And she was living here in Bolton. And I came up and met her and two years later we were married.

JR: And had you already got children?

Joe: Five children, yeah.

JR: So you've not had any together?

Joe: No, they're not mine biologically. No, but they're all my children.

JR: You love them just the same?

Joe: Yeah, when I met them, there were two, four, six and eight. And there's twins. So the twins were two. Boy, four, girl was six and boy eight. And they're now 19, 21, 23 and 26. And they're all brilliant. They're great people.

JR: I did a similar thing and you can make it work, if you want to. It's that old word again, that word want. You know, it creeps into everybody's life. And then you balance it. You balance your role with what they need and what they want.

Let me take you back to your business then, what for the future, Joe? Where are we going with it? With your business, say over the next five to 10 years?

Joe: So we're going for our ISO 9001. So that's quality assurance management systems that are repeatable. We're also commercialising and innovating our service, our products and the way that we do it. So we've got a grant from the government through the E19 fund. And we're putting into place software and AI across our administration and logging and asset management systems.

Not just so that it helps the team, but it'll also help the volunteers and placements use the systems that we use as well. So we're having an AI embedded system to help unify everything across Recycle IT's core processes. Whilst we're working with the Bolton family in Bolton colleges and libraries, we're collecting a lot of equipment and we're placing a lot of the community in a position where they can recycle and refurbish it with us.

And then we can make that available to the community out. So the future is very well mapped out. We'd like to see, ultimately, we'd like to see Recycle IT socially franchised in other towns, in other places. I think this is such a great idea and such a great model.

Every business owner thinks their own model is a great one. But the key metric in this one is everybody else says this is a really good model as well. And I'd love to see this in other parts of the country and other parts of the world, where the community are the recyclers and they learn and they work in synergy.

JR: Let me ask you one last question, Joe, if I may, and it's a very simple question. Do you see your ADHD as a benefit or a negative?

Joe: A benefit. It's a superpower. And I have so much energy. So I have so much encouragement. I have so many ideas around. I'm teaming with them and I have to have mentors and people come in that actually ground me and make those in a reality. Make actionable things and keep me on track.

I'm 54 years old and I feel like a 13-year-old. One of the mentors that I had through the Human Lending Library, Karen Lynch from Bellew Water, she told me to find something that I'm good at and to do something good with it.

JR: And that is exactly what this is. Exactly right. That sums it all up in a sentence. So let me close by saying thank you very much, Joe. Absolutely wonderful to talk to you. Till the next time, eh?

Joe: All right. I'll see you on the next one.

Chapter 9

Vinnie

Some people find their way into prison through a series of bad choices, others through circumstances beyond their control. For Vinne, it was a complex mix of both. His story is one of survival—through a turbulent childhood, loss, self-destruction, and ultimately, a fight for justice and understanding.

Growing up between two households in Wolverhampton, Vinnie's early years were marked by instability, violence, and rejection. School was a battleground rather than a place of learning, and by the age of 14, he had walked away from formal education altogether. What followed was a whirlwind of club life, drag performance, substance use, and personal loss—most devastatingly, the suicide of his closest friend at 21, an event that shattered him and sent him deeper into self-destruction.

But his story is not just one of hardship—it's a story of awakening. His time in prison was not about punishment in the traditional sense. Instead, it became a place where he gained clarity about the injustices faced by neurodivergent individuals in the criminal justice system. Diagnosed with ADHD and autism, Vinnie came to understand not only his own struggles but those of countless others trapped in a system that fails to recognise or accommodate their needs.

Today, Vinnie is a powerful voice for change. He speaks out about the disproportionate incarceration of neurodivergent individuals, the failures of the prison system, and the urgent need for reform. His lived experience has given him a rare and vital perspective—one that challenges the ignorance and systemic failures that keep so many people trapped in cycles of punishment rather than rehabilitation.

This is a story of resilience, raw honesty, and the fight for a fairer system. Vinnie has endured more than most, but he refuses to let his past define him. Instead, he uses it as fuel for change.

The Interview . . .

JR: So welcome and thank you. Now, the purpose of the story is to find your route into jail, what you've done with your life before you went to prison, during your time in prison and what you've left with and where you're going now, because you're not an old man, are you? So you've got a big chunk of your life left to live yet. So I'd like to get an idea.

Was prison a success for you? Did it turn you into a better man and give you a job to come out to? Was it something that spoiled your life and ruined it? And you'll never be the same again? Or what was it? So let's start off with the simplest of questions. You know, growing up, did you grow up with mum, dad, siblings? How was your family situation as a child?

Vinnie: I grew up between two houses. So my mum was in Tettenhall and my dad was in Bushbury. My dad, he rented a house off a notorious Wolverhampton gangster and I didn't have a bedroom in either. So it was a bit fucked up and it was a bit well, it was very unhappy.

It was very violent. So, yes, I didn't really see my siblings. They got pushed out. They were my half-brothers. So when I came along, I was a bastard, but born in wedlock, and I came to destroy.

JR: And what have you got, brothers and sisters?

Vinnie: I've got two brothers. I've got my mums, two half-brothers and two half-sisters.

JR: Do you keep in touch with them now? Or are they not part of your life?

Vinnie: My middle brother, he emigrated to America about 30 years ago. So I have no communication with him since then. My middle sister I speak to, we're rebuilding a relationship. But my other sister, she got me locked up by committing perjury. And my brother didn't help me not get locked up by just giving the silent treatment and allowing the world to take me down.

JR: So this is not a happy family situation?

Vinnie: No, we're a bunch of hysterical psychopaths. OK. Intertwined with neurodivergence. Sorry.

JR: Did you go to school on a regular basis?

Vinnie: I went to school up until 14.When I got to secondary school in year 6, I was asked if I wanted to do my GCCs early. So that's a few years early. And I said no, I wanted to do it at the same time as everyone else because I didn't want to be different.

But I was, obviously. And I stayed till 14. Didn't do my GCCs, but I did get kicked down the science block stairs and beat up a lot. So I started drinking. And one day I was targeted in the wood while I was drinking over lunchtime. And I just thought, I'm not going to go to school again.

So I caught the bus into town and carried on drinking.

JR: OK. And what age was that, 14?

Vinnie: Yeah.

JR: OK. And what did you do with your time after that then? Because you're a relative young man, aren't you? A teenager with plenty of free time. What did you do with your time?

Vinnie: I drank, and I had promiscuous sex. I didn't really take drugs. Not at that point. And I lied about my age so I could start working in pubs and became a drag queen.

JR: Oh, OK. Interesting choice.

Vinnie: So I had a mentor from about 14 who was an 80s dancer and an artist. He ran a club in Birmingham called Money Pennies in the 90s. And put it this way, boy George used to go around his mum's to get ready with him. And his mum would shout to him and boy George, "watch my lino with those heels". Yeah.

JR: So that was your lifestyle, working in pubs, did they also give you somewhere to live? Because I know they used to years ago, didn't they?

Vinnie: The second pub I worked in, yeah. It was a gay bar. So I lived above it and worked beneath it.

JR: You had a home of sorts.

Vinnie: I did, yeah. It was a drugs den, but it was a home.

JR: Yeah, and you had a roof over your head. You had an income and you were working. You were in the dry. Food was available. How many people would survive all of this without too much damage to their life?

Vinnie: Yeah, so from 17 to 20, yeah, that was my life.

JR: OK. Were you on drugs at this point or not?

Vinnie: Yes. Yeah. Double dropping ecstasy. OK. I mean, ecstasy was ecstasy. Ketamine was the big thing then. So I was... Yeah, I can toss a pancake in that ket hole. So they put me to the test.

Everyone was sitting on the floor, unable to move. And at one point, maybe two days later, someone would go, I'm hungry. Can you cook something? So I would hobble off to the kitchen and I thought it was entertaining, to come in and toss a pancake on ketamine. I mean, I was cooking in the kitchen.

Yeah. So I literally, I must be the only person, it could be a world Guinness record or whatever they call it, to be able to toss a pancake on anaesthetic. It was an out of body experience.

JR: You obviously have a very light hearted view of life.

Vinnie: I have, yeah.

JR: And at that age, was that part of the downfall? Was that part of the reason that you were never spurred on to great things? Most people would be looking at careers and marriage and setting down with a family.

Vinnie: No, but I never, I never wanted to have the heterosexual lifestyle, shall we say. So I had, it was my own little family there, if that makes sense.

JR: Were you comfortable?

Vinnie: I was, yeah, but it was a chaotic but exciting and adventurous time. I was very well known for what I did and I was a face in Wolverhampton. And then my best friend a year later, he hung himself. So that is what obstructed me from progress from there.

JR: I understand that, yeah. So how old was he and how old were you when this happened?

Vinnie: We were both 21. He was a couple of months younger than me.

JR: What were the circumstances? Did you find him or did you see this was going to happen? Tell me about his suicide, please.

Vinnie: We were best friends and I was, I suppose we were a bit in love with each other but both were not able to fully express it. He had a partner. He had an unstable home life as well and his mum drank. I didn't want to push him out of a relationship or into a relationship.

I just was there for him and he was, I knew he was depressed and we went out one night and he said, I think I love you too much. And I said, how can you love someone too much? He said, I'm only happy when I'm with you. He went on a depression and I had a phone call from his brother asking if he was with me.

I said no and then a few hours later I had another phone call and I said, he's dead, isn't he? And he said, yeah, he's hung himself. So how it turned out, a bloke with his falcon had gone out and the falcon had gone off. So the bloke went to look for his falcon and the falcon had landed on his shoulder, on his hanging body.

JR: So that's how people were alerted that he'd done it.

Vinnie: Yeah.

JR: Where was this, in an open space somewhere?

Vinnie: Yeah, it was in a beautiful wood, Essington woods.

JR: So he chose the spot?

Vinnie: Yeah. He was very, yeah, he loved Japanese stuff and there's a big suicide forest in Japan. So I think he was, he was close to that. He'd had an argument with his mom and left the house with leaving everything and didn't come back.

JR: OK, very sad event in your life. How did it leave you feeling about life?

Vinnie: I didn't care anymore. I was very self-destructive from that point on.

JR: And you thought, there's no future, can't see where my life's going. Or is that too strong a way of putting it?

Vinnie: No, I was just completely, I was, I was clinically depressed. But I think some, I just, I just drank. I drank or I slept. OK. OK.

JR: So you're not alone doing this, are you? Lots of people do this. So are you under the heading of an alcoholic at this point?

Vinnie: No, I've never been an alcoholic. That's the thing, I've chosen drink as a form of self-medication to deal with anxiety, to deal with social anxiety later on. But to deal with, just to deal with things. But after Josh killed himself, I'd forced myself out and to be some, to be somebody resembling me, I had to drink, or I'd be horrible. In the end, I'd be horrible anyway.

JR: I've lost in my life three people to suicide over a very long period of time. First one when I was late teenage years, about 18 or 19. I'm 36 now, so we're going back a few weeks.

A young lady who I thought a lot of. She wasn't a girlfriend. She was a friend who was a girl. And she committed suicide one weekend. I found at the time that I couldn't relate to it at all. I couldn't understand anyone doing that. And I think part of that was my age and my naivety.

Then I lost, only a few years later, I lost an uncle, which hit me very much harder because he was my favourite uncle. My dad was one of three boys and he was my favourite uncle by a long way.

And he got struck down with depression at the end of his working life. And in the end, he hung himself in his own home and his son found him one morning.

The last one was about five years ago now when a guy that I knew reasonably well from a commercial perspective, he was an estate agent actually and I used to work for him, took a shotgun, went into the field and shot himself.

And on every occasion, I felt that I wish I could have done something about it. I wish I could have seen it coming and help them through it. But of course you can't.

No, this was the big issue. After he did it, on the last day of summer, so the 31st of August comes each year. And, you know, it's like the old story, the Greek story of Demeter mourning Posphona.

And winter comes because she's mourning. I think she died. So I'm sorry, I forgot what on earth I was on about then.

Vinnie: This wasn't my first experience of suicide either. My mom attempted suicide in front of me at six. So, yeah, my mom and my dad were arguing and she went into the kitchen, she overdosed on a heart tablet, and the doctor had given her antidepressants, which she shouldn't have, she's got personality issues. She took all the tablets, came out of the kitchen and collapsed on the floor. So my dad thought she was just drunk at first and it was more interested in the football than her showing up.

So I tried to keep her awake and try to call the ambulance and he took the phone off me and put it down. So she survived. But he did tell me after they took her that she wasn't coming back. But she did. So it was like history repeating. Yeah. And I spent 10 years after Josh did it thinking I've let him do that.

And I haven't, I could have, why did I leave him be? But in reality, there's nothing you can do, is there? I actually shredded a lot of ego at that time. I think because I was, you know, the reason I was, it was selfish. I was doing it for my own benefit, not his benefit and leaving him alone.

JR: So when did the criminal career start then?

Vinnie: Well, seven years after Josh passed away, I'd actually stopped taking the drugs and things and I'd become myself again. And I hadn't been myself for a very long time. Maybe even before Josh, because of drinking drugs. So sober me, I realised it's absolutely terrifying for people and I'm that switched on and I'm that alert and I am fearless and completely able and people didn't like it.

But they saw such a change that they thought it was a negative change. But it was my spirit breaking free. It was a spiritual crisis after so much trauma. Me making this decision to escape abuse of every kind, including medication and labels placed on me by narcissistic abusers. And I fell out with my mum. She told me that I can't go around changing things in other people's lives because I'd attempted to protect someone from being hurt like I had been hurt.

And all the abusers closed ranks and tried really hard to section me first. And when that failed because I wasn't mad, they used the criminal justice system by making false allegations. So I was arrested several times in 2017 and eventually charged with something. And it was something I hadn't done. It wasn't a crime. My crime was freedom of speech. I'd spoken out online against crime and abuse to prevent and detect crime. There was some perverting the course of public justice, shall we say. Some false reporting.

So I was charged with something that was a crime. I got accused of sending stuff but actually it was somebody else who'd sent it to the person and then they'd reported that they'd received it from me. They all knew what each other was doing.

It was highly coordinated. It was extremely sophisticated and desperate because although they said they felt endangered from me, they weren't physically endangered. They felt endangered their reputation. They imagined reputation mixing up their personality with their personas. Abusers don't often realise they're abusers because of what they're doing. They're doing it for an outcome.

This was just an outcome that desired and needed abuse. So I was charged with malicious communications conveying false information that caused serious alarm and distress. But it could also be described as satire. It could also be described as art. It could also be described as opinion. It could be described internationally as freedom of speech.

So I did eight months for that in HMPPS Birmingham. And I got ME so eight months in HMPPS Birmingham didn't do me great.

JR: When was this, Vinnie?

Vinnie: This was between it was October the 11th, 2017 until May 2018 remanded.

Yes, I was remanded for eight months and then when it came to trial I was convicted for 12 weeks. So I'd served like many times that. So I was released to go to back to Brighton where I'd escaped. So I was living on a boat in Brighton. So I'd gone back there and then I was called back.

JR: And was that the end of your criminal career?

Vinnie: No, I was called back. I did 15 months. I was remanded after that and then three years in prison.

JR: And you've not been back since?

Vinnie: No, no.

JR: No, well that's good. You sound like a bitter young man, if I might say that. And for good reason, I might add. I'm not suggesting you're wrong. By any means, you sound like somebody that's had, through life, a really bad deal. Things haven't gone your way.

Choices and chances, if you like, haven't worked for you. They've worked against you. And I wonder, given the story you've just told me, how do you feel now? How do you view the future? What are you going to do? Because what age are you now, Vinnie?

Vinnie: I'm 36 coming.

JR: So you've got a good 30 years, at least, of work left in you. Is there a desire to work? Is there an ability to work? Is there a need to work? Where are you going to go with your life now?

Vinnie: Well, prison gave me one thing. It made me a first-hand witness to injustice and the reality of what prison life is like and how people are treated, how this country treats people. And it made me ultra-aware of my own difference. So all my life, I'd been separated from people, essentially, or mixed with people who were different. And, like, you know, even being a Grebo and a Goth in my youth, you know, we all aimed to be the same type of person, listen to the same music.

Anyway, I was isolated from family, so my ways and my mother's ways were just the ways how people were. But being in prison, surrounded by people and being under constant scrutiny and everyone being under constant scrutiny of myself, it made me ultra-aware of my neurodivergent differences and my family's. And I suppose that makes me a natural psychologist to understand people because I'm not understanding from a normal perspective.

I'm understanding from one of... It's like the allegory of the cave. Are you familiar with that, the philosophical story? I'd spent my life seeing figures walk past a room in which I was kept. And all that was in my life was a fire burning.

And it wasn't until 28 years later I realised that people hadn't been walking around. It had been one person tricking me, holding a silhouette puppet up and walking past. And in the firelight it cast all these shadows on the wall that distorted my idea of reality.

So in prison, having learned my own reality and entering a different reality, a pure, raw reality, I met it with great empathy. And because of my unusual upbringing prison wasn't a place of fear or a place of punishment. I wasn't there to be... I was there to be punished, but I wasn't being punished because I hadn't done anything.

It could do anything to me. It wouldn't be punishment. And because of what environments I was used to, it was exceptionally tolerable.

So I had a unique strength, intelligence and ability that gave me purpose in there to help others. And I left, and I didn't stop needing to help them. So I've worked really hard to raise awareness of the disproportionate prevalence of neurodivergent conditions, especially ADHD and autism, in prison.

The criminalisation of disability. IPP sentences. People in prison on those sentences. They shouldn't be there. They should have been released over 10 years ago instantly. And, you know, that's torture.

If these things aren't spoken about in the public domain every day, like people experience inside every day, then the world won't recognise it, know it, understand it, and know that there's an issue.

JR: I couldn't agree more. I think you've got a very good point. And I think the difficulty becomes how do you make people listen to the argument? I think it's important if you see it to do something about it. Just because everyone's doing it doesn't mean it's the right.

But is anybody listening? Is anybody taking note of what you're saying? And you're right to say it, but is it producing any improvements in the system that will reduce or get rid of completely what you're complaining about?

Vinnie: It is. It's taking away the excuse of ignorance people have to treat prisoners badly. So prison officers with authoritarian personality types, narcissistic personality types. Narcissism is so common in today's society everywhere. In prison, it's no different.

And people who are attracted to those jobs often seek power in some format. And that's what attracts them. That job being of that power dynamic fulfils something in the need of the narcissist.

So without the understanding of neurodivergence, people's behaviour can be judged to be criminal, misbehaving, controllable, just nasty. And they can be punished for it. But with the understanding that neurodivergence exists and emotional dysregulation, the need for structure and routine and sensory overwhelm, sensory sensitivities, with that understanding, those harmful types can no longer do what they're doing.

So when I write something, I know that HMPPS take note of it because they attach it to training programs and documents as links available on the computers of probation and HMPPS. So what I've said in a meeting or what I've spoken to about, you know, they've asked me questions, I've told them my experience, I've discussed ADHD and sensory processing difficulties. That's always there to go back to.

It starts in a conversation because sometimes people have not thought about it. The simple fact is a lot of probation people, they may have worked there a year, 10 years, maybe 20 years. They've never thought about it and they're starting to.

JR: Yeah, they are. It's a long road. I've got every sympathy with what you're saying.

So out of this conversation, which is coming to an end now, out of this conversation comes a very simple reality, I believe, and that is that we're not talking about neurodivergence, especially in prisons, which is our interest, our joint interest, anything like enough. And until we do, we can't overcome the problems that that situation throws up. So we need to wake people up to the existence of neurodivergence and the support that those people need and the help they can get to overcome the problems associated with it.

Some people, of course, call it their super strength, don't they? Well, yeah, it's, they are their disabilities because their differences, you know, maybe everything's designed wrong, maybe everything's designed for someone who's normal, shall we say, or neurotypical. If there is something. Things aren't designed, so maybe it's just how things are designed that are disabling.

There's many ways to look at it, but, you know, there's some people who are very, very disabled, no matter what environment, but even more so in prison. Yeah. I just want to finish just with that understanding that if we just relied on the existence of neurodivergent peoples in the community, to understand neurodiversity, we'd understand it ten times less efficiently than if we did it with people in prison, because there's ten times more neurodivergent people in prison than in the population.

Yeah. And that's, that's the, that's shocking. Of course it is, yeah, of course it is.

I could talk to you forever, Vinnie, but I'm not going to.

Thank you so much Vinnie, a real eye opener.

Chapter 10

Ed

Eddie Flanagan's story is one of survival, transformation, and ultimately, redemption. His life has taken him through the darkest corners of addiction, crime, and institutionalisation, but his journey didn't end there. Instead, it led him to a life of purpose—helping others break free from the very cycles that once held him captive.

Growing up in a working-class London family, one of eight children with an absent father and undiagnosed dyslexia, Eddie quickly became marginalised. By the age of 14, he had already found himself drawn into crime, alcohol, and drug use. What followed was 35 years of addiction and 20 years inside the prison system, where he became institutionalised and deeply embedded in the criminal subculture.

But Ed's story isn't just about crime; it's about resilience and reinvention. Inside prison, he discovered his artistic talent, using it as both a means of survival and a form of expression. His ability to create detailed portraits gave him financial independence behind bars, allowing him to exist outside the typical constraints of the prison economy.

Yet, prison itself did not rehabilitate him. The turning point came when he made the decision to take control of his life. Through the 12-step programme, Ed found the strength to fight his addictions—a battle he continues to face every day. Today, he dedicates himself to working with prisons, schools, and addiction recovery programmes, using his own experience to help others make better choices.

This conversation is a raw, honest reflection on the realities of prison life, addiction, and the challenges of rehabilitation. Ed's journey proves that while the road to change is never easy, it is always possible.

The Interview . . .

JR: My subject matter today is a gentleman called Eddie Flanagan. Eddie Flanagan is a man with an extremely coloured history and an extremely interesting history, and somebody who you wouldn't normally meet except on a place like this, so I work with Ed and do lots of things which he'll tell you about as we go on.

I have the advantage of knowing your life story to a certain extent, but the most important thing, I think, that people would like to hear about is your criminal career. Now, that's not to shine a light on it and make you seem some kind of hero, some kind of man who's gone through life and been tremendously successful, because I know you've said to me in the past, I was never any good at it, John, that's why they kept catching me, but tell me, how did you get into crime, Ed, how did it all begin?

Ed: I come from a working-class background in London, I'm one of eight kids, my father wasn't around, he was an alcoholic. At the age of 12, I started to be sexually abused by a so-called friend of the family.

I started school, I was dyslexic, it wasn't diagnosed in those days, so I became marginalised, so I started hanging about the streets, and by the age of 14, I was committing crime, drinking and taking drugs. That spiralled into 35 years of addiction, 20 years within the prison system, and as an adult I became institutionalised up to the age of 50.

JR: There will be very few people here who will relate to that upbringing. Can you cast your mind back to the first time, maybe at the age of 12 or so, the first crime you ever committed? Did you, for example, go into Woolworths and pinch some sweets, or something like that?

Ed: Yeah, when I was a kid, maybe the odd sweet or two. But it was really when I got into booze and drugs, so age 15, I started to commit my offences, and I was obsessed with motorbikes, so I used to steal performance bikes with an older person. I learnt how to ride a motorbike, and we were selling the engines to people on the racing club circuits around England So at a very early age, I became involved with older criminals and soon got into very serious criminal offending.

JR: Would you say that was a training course, as it turned out?

Ed: Oh yes, yeah. As soon as you go to prison, then you then become part of the subculture that is the criminality within any social system, really.

JR: And how was that first prison sentence, you know, when you first got sent down?

Ed: Terrifying, you're put into an environment that you have no knowledge

of, and even though I was naughty, and I was hanging about with naughty people on the streets, age 16, I got put on remand in Ashford Detention Centre.

Now, every youngster in England before the age of sort of 18, or 21 if you're a prisoner, you will go to a junior prison, and they're even worse than the adult prisons. And there's a lot of bullying, so you have to grow up very quick, and you gain an education in criminality.

JR: Do you mean Ashford in Middlesex?

Ed: Yeah.

JR: Well, a very small world, because that's the town I grew up in. That's where I went to school, and that's where I lived until I got married in 1970, so it could have been you were in the detention centre while I was outside making a living.

Ed: Yeah, probably were.

JR: What a very small world, isn't it?

And it simply progressed from there. Now, I know from previous conversations that there was one aspect of your life that really stood you out from other prisoners when you were inside, and that is your ability to produce art. Now, would you like to tell us a little bit about how that came about?

Ed: Well, creative mediums, I've always been interested in creating. I'm dyslexic, so I think that actually helps me be a better artist, because you find other ways of expressing yourself. And when I was in prison, I taught myself guitar. I was a musician, songwriter, but I could also do portraits.

So, I could earn a living within the prison system, within the prison. I did portraits for staff, for inmates, and obviously I charged them. That allowed me to be independent and to be financially independent, because within the prison system, you are kept under control with the fear of losing what little privileges you have, i.e. your prison wage, in order to buy some goodies, and if you smoke, then to smoke the tobacco.

So, if normal people broke the rules, they would suffer financially, and that stopped them. I didn't have that restraint, because I could earn my own living.

JR: And the other prisoners would pay you for doing portraits of them?

Ed: Yeah, I used to do pencil drawings, and I've drawn everything, from people, to pets, to houses, to cars, you name it, I've drawn it. And it's very important, when you're in prison, you have very, very few personal effects. You would be allowed some photographs of your children and your wife, or your girlfriend, or whatever, but they'd be very small pictures, because of security rules, so nobody could turn them into ID, fake IDs.

So, they would be smaller than your average pictures, but they would be photographs. So, I would then do portraits from very small pictures, and then they could have a life-size portrait of a particular person, or pet, or whatever, hanging on their wall. So, they were very personal, everybody wanted them, and it's very sentimentalised.

There are not many things that get discussed by criminals, but children and families outside, that's the weak point.

JR: At the end of the day, they're all humans, like you and I, it's a subculture. Within our normal society, there's a criminal subculture. We're all aware of it, the only people who live it are the criminals, but society in general is aware of that subculture.

Ed: Yeah. It's the same in prisons, it's a subculture, and you have the rules of the prisons, but more importantly, there's the rules of the prisoners, and what's acceptable amongst them, and that's completely separate to the prison regime.

JR: So, what you're telling me about your life and your time in prison, I can't help but think it is very similar to a business environment.

You ran your drawing service as a business, and so you learnt not only the drawing of drawings that you did, but also how to make money out of it, and how to exist on that money within the limitations of a prison.

Ed: Yeah. Well, the three main currencies, it's a bit old-fashioned now, and it's changed slightly, but in my day, the main currencies was money cash, i.e. £10, £20 notes. This is in the 1970s and 1980s. So, your visitor would come in, they would make it as small as possible, and you would hide it, being polite. You would hide it.

If they covered it in cling film, you would take it back in through orifices. Either you'd swallow it, or you'd stick it up your bum.

JR: Well, don't elaborate anymore, let's get off of that.

Ed: I know that sounds really strange, but if anyone's done any time in prison, that's called the safe, and the word for it is "bottling".

So, yeah. So, the main currencies on the black market in there was money cash, tobacco, because everybody smokes, and cannabis. At that time, it was just cannabis within the prison system.

JR: Okay. So, if you had any of those three, you had a position, maybe not of power, but definitely of more stability than most people. You were maybe more comfortable.

Ed: Yeah. Oh, exactly. So, I used, I would do portraits, I'll get paid in these items, and then I'd invest it in whatever cannabis was on the wing, I'd buy it all up, wait for everything to go dry when nobody had nothing, and I'd put out smaller deals and make money that way.

JR: Fantastic. And this stood you in good stead when you came out of prison. So, would you say that other than acquiring these skills of running a business in prison, the prison experience, was there any major benefit to you? Did it train you to do anything useful?

Ed: Well, if there was suddenly to be a world war, I'd be well equipped to deal with it. But apart from that, I can't really think of any advantages. I'm a survivor. You find out if you're a survivor or not.

And within the prison system, you're either a victim or a fighter, and I was a fighter. A fighter, yeah.

JR: Let's talk about rehabilitation, clearly you are away from this old life now, but how did that happen ?

Ed: Rehabilitation is not only necessary, and the right of everyone who requests it, but for society it is necessary so as to reduce the effect of any particular "bad choice".

The vast majority of people live or experience the kind of life I have had, in many different forms because the human in us all is more conventional. But humans respond to and reflect their surroundings. I was born into a family with little fatherly influence, little money, and nobody to notice and take action over my Dyslexia. This is not to excuse it, but to explain it in a simple way.

JR: The bottom line is, anyone can make a success of their lives if they see the chances offered and make the right choices. For example, in school bullying was very common, it can happen to anyone and is not to be ashamed of or worried about.

Ed: In prison I made a choice that I was not prepared to be bullied, by anybody. This, many would say, was a bad choice, because it required me to meet force with force. But I was in survival mode, so it followed quiet naturally.

Bullies can be rehabilitated, but unless somebody highlights the problem then nothing can be done, knowledge is everything.

But in the prison world rehabilitation takes on a whole new meaning. Take my addiction for example. If, when addicted to alcohol, it had been suggested to me that I should "simply stop" then this would have been almost impossible for me to do. Likewise with any other addiction, your brain works in strange ways sometimes.

JR: So what if you are in prison, due to an addiction, how can you stop ? By "due to an addiction" I mean, what if you are in prison for theft, and that thieving life became necessary to provide the money you needed to finance your addiction ? Would that make it easy to give up ?

Ed: Yes, in prison if I could not get drugs or alcohol then clearly I had no choice other than leaving an addiction in this way (known as "cold turkey"). But since I was not rehabilitated then on release the addiction would return, along with my ability to get money to pay for it.

JR: In Birmingham the Police have a programme that is very helpful. It addresses the problem of addiction and shop lifting at one and the same time. Once an addict wants to give up their habit he or she is admitted into a clinic that takes them through a process that removes the addiction, and in so doing removes the criminal need. The programme is very successful. This is real rehabilitation but is not commonly available.

In conclusion, rehabilitation is only possible when the potential recipient is willing to accept the solution. By far the best path through life is to make the right choices when those chances come along.

Ed: Rehabilitation, using the twelve-step programme, is the only real way of "kicking the habit" and I have worked diligently with others over many years as part of my ongoing rehabilitation programme. In truth, my ability to stay away from alcohol and drugs is still a battle every day and will be until I die. But it is a very worthwhile battle.

JR: But, you know, I would sum up the work that you and I are now doing within the prison service, within the schools network, etc, is absolutely a game changer. And I'm delighted and proud to be a part of it with you.

So, all that remains really, Ed, is for me to say thank you so much for your time today, a story based on what you and I can do and what we do do every day of our lives. So, thank you so much, Ed.

Ed: Bye, everybody. Speak to you soon, John. God bless.

Chapter 11

Ivan

Some careers follow a winding path, shaped by circumstance, personal challenges, and unexpected turns. Ivan's story is one of commitment, resilience, and service—a journey that began in the Royal Navy before leading him into the world of the prison service, where he would dedicate 35 years of his life.

Unlike today's fast-moving job market, where frequent career changes are common, Ivan's trajectory reflects a time when individuals found their calling and stuck with it. His decision to serve in the armed forces was influenced by family tradition, but his later move into the prison system was less planned, shaped by both opportunity and a desire for stability.

However, Ivan's career was not without hardship. A devastating personal loss at a young age shaped his outlook on life and later proved invaluable in his work supporting vulnerable people within the prison system. His journey took him through some of the country's most challenging institutions, from high-security facilities like Belmarsh to prisons dealing with some of the most complex and vulnerable offenders.

Ivan's insights, drawn from decades on the front line, offer a rare and honest reflection on how prisons have changed, the impact of policy shifts, and the vital role that relationships play in rehabilitation and maintaining order. His experiences highlight the stark contrasts between the past and present prison system—where once respect and mutual understanding governed interactions, the rise of new challenges, from staff shortages to organised crime, has created an increasingly volatile environment.

Through it all, Ivan remained steadfast in his belief that prisons should not simply be places of punishment, but of potential transformation. His reflections in this interview are not just the story of one man's career, but a testament to the evolving landscape of justice in the UK, and the enduring need for integrity, humanity, and professionalism within the system.

The Interview . . .

JR: So I'm really interested to talk to you today because although I know some of your life. I don't know all of it So let's make a start. Where were you born Ivan? What was home life like as a child?

Ivan: I was born in in Morecambe Lancashire. My mother was from Scotland and my father was from West Yorkshire They both met whilst serving in the Navy.

My father was in the Fleet Air Arm, serving on HMS Eagle and my mum was working with communications based at HMS Mercury. They met at Lossiemouth naval base.

Lossiemouth's up on the Murray Firth. It's an RAF base now, but it used to be a naval base until the 1970's.

I am one of four children. All four were born in Morecambe. I was initially brought up in Lossiemouth until about 6 years of age. I spoke with a broad Highland accent!

My father left the Navy and joined the Lancashire Police Force. Eventually posted to Morecambe and settling there.

I enjoyed a very normal upbringing. The town was a really good place to grow up in, in the 1960s and 70s. It was an exciting and safe place.

As a family we experienced all of the traditional things including attending the same local schools. I'm the oldest of four John. Two boys two girl's. There's me, my two sisters and a younger brother. Everything really very normal. Money was always tight. We didn't have any luxuries but our clothes were always clean and we never went hungry.

I left school at 15. I left school with 6 "O" levels. Fairly average for my peer group.

I didn't really know what I wanted to do. I had a few ideas kicking around my head. The Navy was obviously something that was very strong in my thoughts. But I really couldn't decide so thought well, I'll go to college for another year. Give myself another year thinking and I'll do some more qualifications and explore viable options for a career.

JR: Did you tell your dad? Did he encourage you or did he say hang on a minute? This is not as good as you might think it is?

Ivan: He didn't want me going in the police. He wanted me to get some life experience under my belt before you considering that. I knew that I was far too immature and lacked life experience anyway. He advised me to consider the armed forces to get a trade and life experience. I had been in the Army Cadets, therefore initially the Army was my preferred option.

The idea of being trained and paid to travel extensively eventually convinced me to join the Royal Navy.

Career opportunities in Morecambe were very limited. The options of further education, going into the building trade or armed forces were pretty much my only options.

Ivan: I enjoyed geography the most at school along with physics, woodwork, photography and English language. I did consider a career with the Forestry Commission. My parents dissuaded me from this (rightly) as the likelihood of going employment was almost nil.

I decided to go to college for a further year to improve my educational qualifications and enable me to better consider a career choice.

However, in mid-1981 my father took his own life. This literally turned mine and my families lives upside down overnight.

JR: Oh, no.

Ivan: Yes he took his own life on a train track at the back of our house.

JR: You can't imagine it can you, unless you've experienced it?

Ivan: No, nothing prepares you for something like that. The whole family went through unimaginable turmoil. There wasn't the support that there is nowadays and there wasn't the appreciation of the impact particularly upon children. In fact, there wasn't any support. So to cut a long story short I just didn't know what to do with myself. I couldn't really think straight so I just decided to join the Navy there and then I thought I just need to get away. I needed to get distracted. I needed an interest. I needed to focus on something other than the immense grief felt by myself and each member of my family. I was weighed down with guilt for leaving my family whilst they needed support for a long time.

Overnight I went from a care free daft as a brush 16 year old to growing up overnight and being required to assume new responsibilities for the family. Mum really suffered but couldn't grieve because she had to hold the family together. My younger siblings suffered terribly. My mothers family mostly lived in Lossiemouth. This made is difficult to provide close support. My father's family did their best living closer in Keighley.

It was a horrendous time for all of the family.

JR: In my lifetime, sadly I've known too many people take their own lives, from children to elderly adults.

I have found that those that actually take their own lives give little or no indication immediately prior to taking their lives.

With each of them I never saw it coming. It just happened. And on each occasion I asked myself what could I have done to prevent that?

Ivan: John, if I had a pound for every minute I've spent going back over and thinking on that fateful day, did I miss something? Did we all miss something? After a lifetime of rumination, I haven't identified anything that could have prevented my father's death.

It's almost impossible to prevent someone taking their own life once they have reconciled their intent. Saying that, I have discussed my personal experience; the impact of suicide on those left behind and viable options with countless numbers of prisoners and some staff. I will never know whether my words and support ever prevented a suicide. I always hoped that they have.

My own personal experience of suicide at a young age has stood me in very good stead in in the prison service and throughout life in better understanding the complexities of mental health and how best to support people in crisis.

JR: But it's worthy of comment I think that that life experience would be something that would serve you well later in life.

Ivan: Oh John, it has served me exceptionally well throughout my life. Hopefully my hard learning that I've sparingly shared with others, staff, prisoners, families and friends alike. As raw and hard as it's been sometimes, hopefully some of that pain has been helpful to others or made other people think about other less extreme options. I like to think John that maybe if just one person considered my experience and learning and then chose a different outcome, then there's been some good come from sharing my experience.

JR: I think you're right and but it's difficult to know isn't it? So how many years were you in the Navy for?

Ivan: Just over six years. I got married at 22. My wife Karen grew up in Morecambe as well. We met when we were both 17. Once we got married she knew that I was committed to the Navy for 22 years. Unfortunately, when we were first married, I was posted away for nine months then I came back for ten days and I was gone again for a further 6 months. So over a period of two years I decided that it was either commit to marriage or commit to the Navy, but It was going to be really tough to commit to both. I decided to leave the Navy and start a new career.

JR: No impossible.

Ivan: Yeah, I didn't want to drag Karen all around the UK and world living on her own. She was very much a homegirl and wanted to be close to her family. It was important to me to make sure that she didn't lose her roots or closeness to her family and friends.

JR: Is Karen the lady you're married to now ?

Ivan: Yes my only wife. We married in 1985. We were both 21.

At 26 I came out of the Navy and did what lots of ex-service people do, I applied for the fire brigade, prison service, police, MOD.

I knew the least about the prison service out of the others.

JR: Tell me what drew you towards it then what was the deciding factor for the prison service?

Ivan: The honest truth John was that there wasn't anything that really turned my head in the beginning. It was a case of applying for a number of things and I just hit the Prison Service at a sweet spot in time when they were mass recruiting in the in the late 1980s. Prisons were very closed places with little public understanding of what went on behind the walls.

My application was almost return by post. I was invited for interview, and it was only then that I started making serious inquiries into what the job entailed. I started looking up and speaking to people that were in the prison service at HMP Lancaster Castle. My interest started to develop from then on. I was offered a prison officer training course at Hull University. I thought right well I've got nothing better to do so I'm going to do that and see how it goes. I did the training course and then like everyone else at that time, the Prison Service said, "write down three prisons and you'll get choice one two or three we can't guarantee which one".

I thought I've come out the Navy to give some stability I will give them a massive choice by stating "anywhere north of Birmingham". They allocated me to the Isle of Wight! There was no appeal in them days. It was a case of you turn up on the day or don't turn up at all.

I wasn't going to accept this posting and was prepared to leave the Prison Service.

Sadly, this was the situation for the majority of people on my intake. The mass recruiting was predominantly London and the South East we found out to all of our cost!

I managed to do a three-way swap and I got HMP Chelmsford down in Essex. Karen said, okay then we'll give it a go so that's what we did. If things didn't work out, I, we, were prepared to return to Morecambe and pursue other options. I was bitten right from the beginning and never looked back for the next 35 years!

It was a really interesting place to work, they hadn't had any new staff for donkey's years. So all these new ultra keen officers joined at the same time. It forged us together and almost felt like a brotherhood. I felt that this was a vocation where I could use my life experienced both before and after the Navy to do some good for others.

JR: Paint me a picture of Chelmsford prison. I've no comprehension of it, I've not been there. But what category is it, and how many men has it got?

Ivan: Going back to those days late 1980s it was a category "A" prison on the outskirts of London, so it had lots of the London prisoners, so lots of the London gangsters serving long sentences. It also served the courts of Essex and had a young offender function. Sewing mailbags was the largest prisoner activity available and there was a bath house where prisoners were escorted to on a weekly basis.

I know that sounds old, doesn't it? They'd recently repaired a big part of the prison after a fire. During the refurbishment the film "Porridge" was made starring Ronnie Barker. If you watch that will give you an idea of what it was about. A Victorian prison in urgent need of modernisation described it well!

Culturally It was a place that was that was really stuck in the dark ages. Staff had been there for donkey's years. Apart from the odd one or two, there had been no new staff until I went in with the large cohort. We were treated appallingly by many peers and managers. I am glad to know that those behaviours are long consigned to history.

There was absolute resentment towards us. We were given all the foulest jobs you can imagine on the basis of being new.

But tempered with that there was an abundance of experience and comradery amongst the new staff. The experience was there, you could go to most people and ask for ideas, ask for solutions, and you got it. Sometimes in unexpected formats. Even the people that I got negative experiences from, I still got learning from them. Because you are learning and developing in your job I was constantly thinking right well, I'm gonna pinch that from him. I'm not gonna do what he's done because I don't like that and you blend it all in with your own beliefs and standards.

My peers and I underwent a huge learning journey acting as a prison officers at that poignant time on the landings, working with convicted male adults and young offenders as the prison service embarked on a course of rapid modernisation.

I experienced some real shocks, many highs and personal achievements. It was a time I remember really fondly even the bad times. I can still look and laugh and think of the camaraderie how everyone stuck together. Even the most abrasive and obstructive peers and manager's softened and became positive role models and some even becoming lifelong friends.

JR: When you look at how chaotic it was, how safe was it ?

Ivan: Ironically, it felt really safe compared to nowadays. We made it safe. We had the staff ratios, time and mutual respect to maintain high levels of safety. There were still too many instances of violence but nothing compared to current levels.

These were the days of slopping out before any in-cell toilet facilities. It was a disgusting and degrading time. The pungent smell that used to hit you when you first walked onto the wings in the morning was indescribable. The smell was absolutely putrid and if you'd been on leave, you know three or four days or a couple of weeks when you came back it was almost overpowering. At the end of each day the reek was in your clothing, hair and skin! It was horrendous.

Some of the awful jobs that you used to get as a new officer would be "shit parcel patrol". You would take a couple of prisoners out and you'd walk around all the outside areas of the wings in a morning and you collect "shit parcels". Prisoners would rather defecate in a newspaper and throw it out the window rather than stink the cell out for their cell mates!

This vile job got much worse during the warmer months!

To think this is in our lifetime, we're not talking medieval times are we? We're talking, you know late 1980s early 1990s. I believe that the very last of "slopping out" only ended in the early 2000's!

If you weren't out on "shit parcel patrol" you were in charge of the sluice areas. Each landing had a sluice area where prisoners would take their night pots and empty them and wash them out. As a new prison officer, you'd be allocated to the sluice areas supervising making sure that nobody was up to any sort of shenanigans. You can imagine you the smells, spills and God knows what else that took place?

JR: Did you find yourself at any risk at that point? I mean it would surely be a fairly easy thing for the prisoner to throw his bucketload of whatever all over you.

Ivan: Yes, like nowadays when you first unlock large numbers of prisoners simultaneously, the risk of violence increases.

"Potting" as it was known as was pretty rare. If it occurred once a week in the entire prison, that would be enough.

Potting of staff or a prisoner was universally seen as the ultimate insult and degradation. Every prison officer and prisoners would say "I would rather be punched than have a pot of faeces and urine thrown over me". It was absolutely horrendous.

In those days the Board of Visitors (IMB) could and would award additional periods of imprisonment for perpetrators of plotting.

JR: Did it happen often?

Ivan: I would say, you know once or twice a week if things were volatile. Otherwise, mercifully quite rare (weekly).

Most prisoners were equally repulsed by the thought of an officer receiving it. There was a mutual understanding between staff and prisoners that It was as horrible as it could get so whilst one occasion was one too many, once a week was about as many as it would be.

Often prisoners would discretely inform staff about a fellow prisoner planning to "pot" someone. We would take appropriate actions to try and prevent this from happening.

JR: Okay, so somewhere in Ivan's life at this point we've got a job that is not the best paid job in the world, we've got a job where you are at some physical risk from the people you're working with, we've got a job that yes, you could be there for the rest of your working days, but whether you would want to be or not is another matter. It's a job where your workmates don't necessarily want you there because they've been there a long time and you're the new incumbent so if you took all those minuses together what was the plus that kept you staying there that made you realise that prisons would be a career that you would enjoy ?

Ivan: It was compounded even more so because in the late 1980s we had the extortionate interest rates for mortgages. A lot of my peers, prison officers that were transferred to Chelmsford and particularly the London and south east areas couldn't afford to live in or near Chelmsford, or their respective prison. We had people living in tents in the staff car park. We had people living in their cars, with washing lines strung out between the cars and the bushes. So it was a really, really tough time. But I saw enough opportunities, I saw career progression and just felt that things would improve in the future.

I saw and liked what I thought was a challenge, this was despite experiencing an unwelcoming culture, financial hardship and some rotten aspects of the new job.

I just thought that most prisoners had a worse hand than I had and I could still do something to help them change and be better members of society.

I recall discussing with my wife that if we can get through the early months and I can do some good, it's worth a punt to hang in there.

JR: So could you say then that that sort of born into you instinct to try and help others and do your best at all times? Which would have served you well in the Navy, of course, wouldn't it? Carried on into the prison service and stood you in good stead for the rest of your working life ?

Ivan: I think that sense evolved, developed and grew with a deeper understanding of the meaning of being able to help others. Whereas before helping others might have been carrying a heavy bag or opening a door or going around to help a mate do some or something.

Now I was helping others that were suffering. Mentally suffering from other things like substance abuse or violence etc. I had a much deeper appreciation and a resonance with me if that makes sense.

I felt able to help people become better individuals which felt an enormous responsibility and privilege.

JR: Yes, it does make sense. Is there is there any one prisoner you can remember, not necessarily to name him, although you can if you want to, that sticks in your mind perhaps somebody anybody reading this book would recognise the name and would see him in a different light to what the popular view would be?

Ivan: Yeah, have had the benefit of meeting many memorable prisoners. Particularly during the 10 years I worked at HMP Belmarsh. I had first had experience with politicians, pop stars, footballers, infamous gangsters, terrorists, actors and heads of international drug cartels.

One of my most abiding memory is that of an elderly prisoner at HMP Gartree. He had been persuaded to attend education in his mid-60's by prisoner education peer mentors. He couldn't read or write. This had contributed directly to his life of crime.

A wonderful tutor persevered with him for almost 2 years. Culminating in him sitting and passing both English and maths exams.

As Governor I routinely presented certificates to prisoner's.

It was humbling and joyful to see the sense of pride in the prisoner, staff and fellow peer mentors when presenting his certificates.

I learnt that these were the first ever certificates this prisoner had ever received and he had no memory of anyone ever praising him for any achievement until this occasion.

This for me epitomises what can be achieved when people work together for the good of others regardless of how unremarkable it may seem.

JR: Do prisoners and staff still share a mutual respect?

Ivan: No, absolutely not John. Sadly, that's largely gone now. I think, and I'm jumping around a little bit here, but in the early days one of the things that I remember very starkly was female prison officers being deployed to male prisons in the in the late 1980s early 1990s and I really thought "this could go one of two ways". But again, going back to what I said earlier, one of the things that I remember really starkly is the extra respect that was given to female staff by the male prisoners.

The way that they would maintain themselves when interacting and even in the presence of female staff showed respect.

They wouldn't swear in front of female staff. They certainly wouldn't get involved in in acts of violence in front of female staff. They would self-police that if someone was behaving in a way that was disrespectful to a female member of staff, peer pressure would be applied and that person would be reprimanded by his own peers.

The same levels of respect would be afforded to elderly members of staff, those with significant prison experience and/or those with a noticeable disability.

Sadly, mirroring much of society now, such the like are all too often viewed as easy targets and a means to an end.

JR: I know exactly what you're saying because the first prison we met in namely Stafford when I was sent into the Senior Support Group cabin where there might be 40 men in together in the one cabin, in two separate rooms, and one little female officer sat at the end, keeping an eye on things, and she was never under any threat. Admittedly, they're all over 65, but nevertheless, had any one of them decided to hurt her or me, could have done, but nobody ever did.

Ivan: HMP Stafford is unique throughout HMPPS. Much of the prisoner cohort is elderly and still retains that respect for those in authority. By no means is this complete.

It was a completely different time in the 1980/90's. Society was different.

The currency in prisons then was a bit of tobacco, phone cards, tea, coffee, sugar and cannabis.

Today it is on an industrial scale in comparison involving organised crime groups trafficking psychoactive substances, hard drugs, mobile phones, modern day slavery and money laundering. The stakes, risks, rewards and consequences for staff, prisoners and their families has changed exponentially.

JR: When you look at the dynamics and complexities to deal with now, it's a different prison system completely.

Ivan: Absolutely. We didn't have the risk of, drugs, we didn't have the risk of mobile phones, you know, we didn't have the risk of psychoactive substances and the levels of staff corruption.

JR: Did you have the same self-harm and suicide rates?

Ivan: No, nowhere near, John. Like a lot of things, there's a lot of nuances there. I don't know if you remember, again in the early 1990s, John, there was massive reform done with mental health in the country.

Essentially, most of the secure mental health support networks and institutions were shut down and people had to be managed in the community. Well, all of a sudden, it literally was overnight, prisons became full of people with severe and complex mental health conditions.

Overnight, instead of managing people that were predominantly criminals we were managing people that had complex mental health problems, chronic mental health problems, because there was nowhere else for them to go. The Courts simply had no options available. None of us were trained in mental health, none of us had an understanding of mental health conditions let alone complex conditions. We didn't have the facilities, we didn't have the training, we didn't have the support networks such as NHS.

All's we had was the physical environment and control and restraint training.

In those days, we had padded cells and some prisons has small in-house healthcare teams.

The forerunner to the ACCT document was something called an F2052SH combined with whatever individual compassion and common sense each of us possessed. It was a horrendous time, John, it was absolutely horrendous, having to look after these really, really ill men, young and old. And so it was a really poor indictment on this nation.

It is only in this past couple of years whereby HMPPS has employed dedicated neurodiversity staff to compliment contracted mental health partners. Front-line staff still do not have adequate mental health training.

JR: So moving on from Chelmsford, then, how long were you there? And where did you go to?

Ivan: I was at Chelmsford initially for five years, because back in those days you had to be a prison officer for five years before you could apply, even apply for the senior officer exam. So once I'd got my five years in, I applied to be a senior officer and I was successful.

Belmarsh opened and I thought, that'll be an interesting challenge.

JR: Did you see Belmarsh as the future?

Ivan: Yeah. So I threw my hat in the ring for Belmarsh on promotion and I got it. I transferred from Chelmsford to Belmarsh and I went on the most amazing 10-year learning journey that I could possibly have ever done.

JR: Tell me about Belmarsh, because I've never been in Belmarsh.

Ivan: At the time, Belmarsh was brand new. It was deemed the flagship of the prison service. All the most dangerous prisoners in the country were concentrated in Belmarsh. Within Belmarsh, there was a unit called this Special Secure Unit. It is 48 cells within its own prison wall, enhanced security systems, and higher than normal staffing levels. It is a prison with a prison.

I was posted there as a senior officer. So my first posting on promotion was to the Special Secure Unit. And it was predominantly occupied by IRA prisoners.

JR: Were they on the dirty protest at this time or was nobody doing that anymore?

Ivan: They were doing dirty protests on a regular basis. Everything, both unpleasant and enjoyable was a huge learning curve for me. There wasn't a day that I went into Belmarsh that wasn't a learning day.

The staff culture was the polar opposite to Chelmsford. It was positive, supportive, equal and united.

I worked in the Special Secure Unit. Then got promoted again after another two or three years to what was then the Principal Officer, which is the equivalent to custodial manager. I really, really enjoyed that grade/role.

This was my ambition when I joined the prison service. I thought, right, I want to be a principal officer.

Principal Officer was the highest grade in the uniform hierarchy. And it operated between governor level and the unified grades.

I was put in charge of an entire wing that had, I think, nearly 200 Category A and escape list prisoners. So, again, it was a challenge, responsibility and learning.

These were exciting times both for Belmarsh and HMPS.

Team ethos there was something I'd never felt before in the prison service, and I never felt afterwards when I left Belmarsh. It was completely unique. This Emirates from the Director General, HQ and Belmarsh.

It was just the time, the type of prison, the people that came there. It was a real exciting period to be. In the prison service. So, all in all, I did enjoyably rewarding years at Belmarsh.

JR: 10 years come to an end. Where did you go then?

Ivan: I'd done 10 years commuting from Chelmsford. I was tired. Tired physically, mentally, and I had neglected my family due to the excessive daily commute.

I needed to give some time back to my family. So, I went back to Chelmsford as a governor grade, head of security. Chelmsford had re-rolled since I'd left it. It was now a Category B local prison. So, serving the courts of Essex.

When prisoners were sentenced/convicted, they were allocated and transferred out. It still had a few Category A prisoners but only short term and a few E-list prisoners.

But it was still an interesting prison because at the time, phones were just coming into prisons. Drugs, particularly cannabis, heroin and cocaine. This was the beginning of prisoners and criminals earning big money in prisons.

HMPS had experienced numerous highly embarrassing security failings. It was a good time to be a security manager and bring about change.

JR: It would be a harder thing in those days to smuggle a phone in than it is nowadays, I take it. Much, much harder.

Ivan: Yes a lot harder, and phones were bigger. People and media weren't as sophisticated. You had more staff to physically search people and property

There was dedicated search teams, dedicated security teams. People that were trained and experienced to a far higher degree. They had more time to do those jobs.

They had more time to develop networks to find out who was doing what, to build intelligence pictures. It was a challenge and things were far from ideal, it was an exciting time to meet those challenges.

JR: Is it as true to say in prison, as they say in the police force, don't they, we can only police by consent ? And is it the same in a prison, do you think, that you can only look after the people in your care with their consent? If they don't give you the consent, then you can't do it.

Ivan: Absolutely, John. Yes that's 100% true. Order and control is largely relevant on prisoners consent, because as history shows, when that consent is withdrawn, then riots ensue, protests, disorder and violence ensues.

The bottom line, John, is that there will always be more prisoners than staff in a prison.

Even in the good old glory days, you were outnumbered four to one on a good day even in Belmarsh.

Fast forward to 2024, you know, staff now are outnumbered up to 25 to one in some prisons.

JR: Crikey. So, yeah, the consent has to be there. And you have to govern by, you know, legitimate authority.

JR: And of course, that's one of the problems of staff turnover, isn't it? That you need to work some kind of a relationship between the prisoners and the officers controlling them. I'm not saying you have to be best buddies, but you certainly have to have a working relationship.

Ivan: John, you've hit the nail on the head. This is one thing that has never changed during all of my time in the prison service. You strip away everything else, everything. Fundamentally, the best work that any prison officer can do is through building a professional relationship with a prisoner.

And that takes time, John. That takes exposure. That takes events, good and bad. That takes trust. That takes mutual respect.

And that was the case when I was a prison officer. It's absolutely the case now. The difference between then and now is that I had the time, I had the opportunities, and I had the staff numbers to build positive relationships with prisoners.

But I wouldn't build relationships with every prisoner because there just wasn't enough time. And there's some prisoners and some staff that you just don't click with. But with a diverse mix of staff, the hope is that someone will form a relationship with every prisoner.

As a collective group of staff, the relationships that develop are known as dynamic security.

Regimes, prison cultures and staff training are but aspects that contribute to good dynamic security. Positive staff prisoner relationships built across the piece between all the staff and the prisoners is vital in order to win their consent. Using legitimate authority is paramount to run a safe, decent, and secure prisons.

When those critical building blocks start being eroded, i.e. you haven't got enough staff per ratio of prisoners, you haven't got the time to expose yourself to those prisoners, to have those discussions, to really understand what's going on in their lives, and to see them behaving naturally, and to challenge where the behaviour is not good, and to recognise where it is good, and to provide the support where it's needed. All of those things and more when diluted to an extent that they are at the moment, is when all of those other aspects around consent, respect, security, safety, decency all become weakened and become in danger of catastrophic falling.

JR: And that's another aspect of the future, isn't it? Because we haven't yet covered when you went from Chelmsford and beyond to when I met you in Stafford. Did you make that journey all in one lump, or is there another prison between?

Ivan: Oh my god, I'll fast forward then. I worked in 13 prisons at different grades and roles. Such experience through the prison system and career structure, is unlikely to be replicated nowadays. This reflects the change in both HMPPS expectations and today's mobile workforce.

JR: Somebody joining as you did at age 28 or 30 or whatever, and spending the next 35 years there, if they do that now, it's very difficult to understand how they could possibly get to the stage that you've got to.

Ivan: I'm not saying one's right or wrong. I can put a strong case for my experience, John, but when you can join the prison service and it is the norm to become a custodial manager in 18 months, I do not see how you can have developed in this most critical grade the knowledge, the experience, the authenticity, the integrity, the reputation to manage a group of staff, to manage a group of prisoners, and to do that in a competent, confident, equal manner.

JR: No, nor do I. So, let's go from Chelmsford to Stafford then, because forgive me going back to Stafford, but it's where you and I met and it's where your career ended. So, how many steps were there between the two? Prisons in many ways are similar, but also in many ways they're very different. So, how do you shape up after that?

Ivan: Okay, I mean, first and foremost, there are a lot of similarities amongst all prisons, but every prison has a different culture, and that culture changes at different times.

So, the culture that was at Chelmsford when I first went was a different culture when I went back 15 years later. So, I went from Chelmsford then to Glen Parva, to Gartree, which was all lifers. I then went from Gartree to Onley, which was a cat "C" training prison.

Then on to Ranby near Doncaster, which was a large cat "C" industrial prison. All the time getting more senior grades, moving up the ladder. I then went from Ranby to Leicester as a governor. So, my first prison as a governor, as in The Governor, was Leicester.

JR: So, I knew Phil Novus at Leicester, were you there before him or after him?

Ivan: Phil came after me. Okay. I replaced Ali Barker who then left. I then went from Leicester to Glen Parva again, prior to it shutting down. I then went from Glen Parva again to Gartree again. And then I went from

Gartree to Swinfen Hall, and then from Swinfen Hall to Stafford. And then from Stafford to retirement.

JR: So, let's talk about Stafford for a minute, because you and I have got a common interest here.

And, you know, many people reading this book will never ever have been inside a prison, let alone a prison that was designed to house, what, 750 men, all of whom have been found guilty of some sexual crime of one way or another. So, you know, it's not exactly rare in our system, but it's unusual, shall we say. And certainly when I went there for the first time, when the governor before you was there, my family certainly had a view of what a prison full of sex offenders might be like.

And it was nothing like what they thought it was. And of course, they'd never been in a prison. So they wouldn't know. It's just a perception. I find in my, much reduced compared to yours, career in the prison service. I've been working in prisons now for what, six, seven years. I found Stafford to be the happiest place I've ever been to. And the gardens are immaculate. The food served by the prisoners in the cafe is wonderful. The bistro, as it's called.

And the people, very pleasant to deal with. So, I mean, the prisoners and the staff. So for me, for you, was it a happy place?

Ivan: Oh, tremendous. And I couldn't think of a better place to finish my career. Because with all the troubles and challenges that the prison service has faced over the past 15 years and continues to face, Stafford for me was an oasis. It reminded me of what prisons were like 15, 20 years ago.

JR: Exactly what you've said there. It was clean. Decency was a priority. It felt safe. Staff were happy. You could achieve things.

Ivan: You know, certainly as a governor, if I wanted, my vision, if I wanted to do ABC. Almost, almost certainly I could achieve ABC. Sometimes, you know, I would have to work a little bit harder to get some things done.

But I could realise my vision. I could set standards and hold people to them. I knew that people coming into work would be relatively safe.

I was exciting to support and encourage both staff and prisoners to get involved in the development of the prison and shape the regime to their own expectations and ambitions.

And that was for staff and prisoners. It was a happy place to work.

People enjoyed coming to work there.

Prisoners felt safe and secure there. Prisoners felt in the main that they could address their offending behaviour. All of those rehabilitative things that developed in me and I enjoyed in my early years in the prison system, that really were, let's say, sidelined for probably the next 15 year period.

It was a good way for me to end my career, reminding myself what prisons can be like. If the environment is conducive with a positive place, life changing work can flourish. It felt like I had travelled full circle.

JR: One of the first things I tell them, apart from the fact that I don't want to know what they're in for or anything like that, I'm not the least interested in the sentence. What I'm trying to develop between the two of us is trust and respect. And it was interesting to me to know your use of these two words previously. Because I believe, and you obviously believe as well, that once you've got those two things in place, you can get a suitable working relationship with almost anybody to their advantage.

It makes them easier to control. And also it makes it easier to provide them the help they need to overcome the reason that got them there in the first place. Because not everybody goes to prison.

So we're not all naughty boys or girls.

Ivan: No, I can't underestimate it, John. And this is something that is probably the most important single item that the service seems to be losing its memory of the critical importance of nurturing good positive professional staff prisoner relationships. The value that comes from this has and continues to be undervalued and under prioritised. It's not just trust, respect, safety, hope, that permeates through to the prisoners' families and their friends. It's creating the enabling environment that facilitates opportunities for rehabilitation.

The corporate memory is fading every year as another year goes by effective staff prisoner relationships are not achieved leaves new and inexperienced staff never having truly experienced the benefits and potential of good staff / prisoner relationships. The truly disturbing danger is that this will get lost forever.

JR: Well Ivan I couldn't agree more and I think we'll close on that point with perhaps me making a closing statement that I wonder, and you're very welcome to comment, I wonder whether one of the reasons we're not getting the corporate leadership nowadays in prisons as we've discussed today is that the people making those rules and regulations, the Government themselves, are getting younger and less experienced and so we're going through a complete change of culture throughout the country and it remains to be seen what comes out on top. But I can't help but feel that the prison of today is not as good as the prison was 20 years ago perhaps.

Ivan: I'd agree with most of that John it depends you know as to what we define as good. It certainly wasn't perfect. It's never been perfect in my entire time you know. Prisons unfortunately are political footballs and there's been some absolute shocking things happened to prisons and Probation by successive governments. Opportunities to rehabilitate and the eye watering amounts of money that's been squandered is just it's scandalous. A root and branch review of the CJS and HMPPS is critical to arrest the spiralling failure occurring.

If you think of what good can be done I do believe John that and this isn't rocket science. As you know this is basically about fellow human beings needing to form healthy relationships and do what is know to work in order that those convicted of crimes are better placed to lead law abiding lives upon their release. The bottom line is if I know you John and I respect and I understand your capabilities and vice versa. Plus I know a little bit about you as a person not just an officer, I'm far less likely to want to hit or hurt you.

I'm far less likely to want to escape or compromise you. I'm far less likely to do anything untoward that's going to discredit you. I'm going to trust and rely upon you. This way, if you tell me that this is what I need to do to address my reoffending I'm going to listen to you and I'm going to invest in you. I'm going to do what you're asking and directing me to do believing that you have your best intentions for me.

These very same things were absolutely true right back when I joined and decades before. It is even more critical nowadays.

I will reiterate my belief that there's a significant number of influential people in both Government and HMPPS that have never experienced the potential of truly investing in those staff prisoner relationships.

They read and hear about dynamic security and it's importance. They'll agree with its necessity and value. Unfortunately, that's where the conviction and commitment ends.

Intent and capability to address over the past two decades has been superficial and half hearted. The shambolic state of the Keyworker scheme is the latest in the crisis cycle.

They'll have read it and it'll be there with everything else that they've read but they don't invest in it John and that that's where we're at with why aren't things working the way they should do because there's lots and lots of rhetoric about "we know what to do" and we know what should be done but actually doing it and knowing what works John and what good looks like that memory is eroding year after year after year.

Because there's old fossils like me and there's still a few kicking around we remember it when it works John the phenomenal benefits for everybody allow you to build the rest of the vision around a prison but if you neglect that part, the relationship part, John, then everything else is built on sand.

JR: Yes I agree absolutely it's a wonderful story Ivan I'm very grateful to you for telling me it I feel I know you a little bit more now so thank you for your time today and we'll close now.

Ivan: thank you John hope I haven't bored you.

In Conclusion

Now retired, this true story serves as a salute to the integrity of Ivan, a man who has chosen his path through life, and followed it come what may, until nowadays when he enjoys a well-earned rest.

A confirmed family man, his example to all of us but particularly his own family, is to be admired.

Stories From the Inside Out

Epilogue

This book began in a completely different format to that which you, my respected reader, have now read and, I hope enjoyed.

Initially, we had the idea of recording the voices of many people who currently are incarcerated and to make that into a podcast for the future. The plan was evolved with the help of the Governor of the prison and with the help of many other people, we put together a series of recordings not only of the residents of this particular prison, but also of the staff that look after and care for these residents.

As time went on, it became obvious that the people we were talking to had a very powerful message. The message they wanted to convey to the public was a simple one, we are people. We respect what is being done for us. Likewise with the staff they had a caring nature and believed that in their hands the residents would come to no harm. They also believed that the outcome of their incarceration would be positive. That people would leave rehabilitated and would not repeat the offences that had put them in prison in the first place.

In reality rehabilitation in prison is rare. The truth of the matter is that there are not enough facilities in any prisons to cope with the numbers of people that are going to need them. Crime is on the increase and given the age of the prisons in the estate and the number of staff that we have it is likely that only around 25% of the population will be able to receive any kind of rehabilitation.

So what is rehabilitation? What is the value of it to society? In simple terms, rehabilitation means that we should help the people in our care to return to society less inclined to continue their criminal career. Less able to repeat the offence for which they have been incarcerated. Less likely to want to live in a prison instead of living in society.

But this would be utopia. We perhaps could close some of our prisons or at least reduce their volume. The cost of running our prisons is huge. Along with staffing costs there are many other costs. Such as maintenance of the building, training and employing staff, food, heating and many other various additional administration costs.

Having read this book. Do you think that rehabilitation is a worthwhile cause? Or do you think that we should lock these people up? That we should leave them inside until their sentence is served and only then release them back into the community. Possibly to commit more crimes. That is a question for another day. And as I complete this book I wonder, where will the next book in this series take us?

Until then . . . John

Printed in Great Britain
by Amazon

58219169R00089